ANCIENT CORINTH
NAUPLION - TIRYNS
MYCENAE - EPIDAURUS

«OLYMPIC COLOR»

JOHN DECOPOULOS

6 APOLLONOS STR. HELLINICO - ATHENS

TEL. 99.13.790 - 99.22.699

 ©

TEXT : KELLY PETROPOULOU - PHOTO : I. DEKOPOULOS

ANCIENT CORINTH

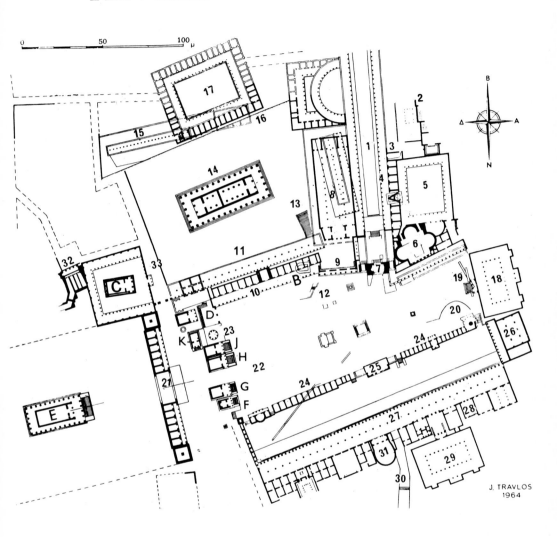

0   50   100 μ

J. TRAVLOS
1964

PLAN OF CORINTH

1. Lechaion Road — 2. Baths of Eurycles — 3. Public Lavatories — 4. Roman Shops — 5. Perivolos of Apollo. **A. Greek Temple.** 6. Peirene Fountain (Lower) — 7. Triumphal Arch — 8. North Basilica — 9. Captives' Façade — 10. North West Shops — 11. North West Arcade (Stoa). **B. Greek Temple.** 12. Wall with Triglyphs and Sacred Spring — 13. Staircase — 14. Temple of Apollo — 15. Commercial Arcade — 16. Greek Bath — 17. North Market — 18. Julian Basilica — 19. Starting line — 20. Retaining wall — 21. Western Shops — 22. Roman Temples (D. K. J. H. G. F) — 23. Monument of Babbius — 24. Central Shops — 25. Bema (Rostrum) — 26. Tabularium (South East Building) — 27. South Stoa — 28. Office of the Agonothetes — 29. South Basilica — 30. Kenchreai Road — 31. Vouleftirion (Senate) — 32. Glafki Fountain. **C. Temple of Akraia Hera. E. Temple of Octavia.** 33. Sikyon Road.

PREHISTORIC - HISTORIC

On the northern foothills of Acrocorinth, set upon the ruins of the ancient Greek town, there is today a small village, Old Corinth. In contrast, the town which bears the name Corinth (New) is built in the recess of the Gulf of Corinth and dates back only as far as 1858. At that time, after a devastating earthquake, the inhabitants who had succeeded the ancients, the Byzantines and the post-byzantine generations, always living on the same land, began building a new city, 6 kms farther down and nearer the sea, this time.

Although in the memory of the later generations the history of the wealth of the ancient Greek city alone lived on, the suffix «nthos» (Korinthos) reveals a pre-hellenic origin. Excavations proved that the site of the ancient city as well as certain other points in the province of Corinth, rich in water and vegetation, had been inhabited from very old times, in fact 7,000 years ago (Neolithic Age).

With time, the first prehistoric settlements began to grow in number and their civilization, which passed from the stone age to the bronze age, evolved in a natural manner until the beginning of the second millenium B.C. when the first known Greek speaking tribes descended into Greece. At about that time, some natural disaster appears to have caused not only the desertion of the settlement at Corinth but also of those in the surrounding district, such as Korakou, Gonia, etc. Despite all this, life continued, even if only in a conventional manner for another thousand years. In fact, shortly before the end of the 13th century B.C., the inhabitants of Corinthia built a powerful cyclopean wall, a section of which was discovered on the eastern side of the isthmus. Possibly this wall constituted part of defences put up to ward off an invasion from the north.

Between 1125 and 1100 B.C., the first groups of Dorians crossed over into the Peloponnese across the Straits of Rion. Fifty years later, with some considerable delay in colonizing Corinthia, a particular Dorian group under Aletes of the royal house of the Vakhiades, settled themselves in the area.

The new settlers who arrived aboard ships which sailed from the Maliakos Gulf (east central Greece), first occupied the Solygio hill a few kms south of the Isthmus and only a short distance from the sea. It was not long, however, before Acrocorinth won their preference. It occupied a privileged position and was a naturally fortified point, useful in the event of an enemy raid. It controlled the way into the interior of the Peloponnese and from there the rest of mainland Greece. Thus life returned to the deserted land and was destined, in a remarkably short time to attain great prosperity. By the 8th century B.C. Corinth had come to count among the most important Greek cities. It was about the time when centrifugal forces began to develop in the Greek world. In company with Euboea and the Cyclades Islands, Corinth took part in the second wonderous operation of the second Greek colonization. Already, since the 9th century B.C. when a small colony was established in Ithaca, Corinth blazed the trail to the west. One after another, Corinthian colonies sprang up. Among the more important were Corfu (734 B.C.) and Syracuse in Sicily. Maritime operations as dangerous and distant as these required not only seafaring experience but also a degree of progress in the art of shipbuilding. It is no mere coincidence that the first known European shipbuilder was Ameinocles the Corinthian who, in 704 B.C., built ships on order for the island of Samos.

The colonies gave trade a great boost. Corinthian ships set sail from the port of Kechreai on the shore of the Saronic Gulf to go east and fetch essential oils and perfumes. These were later processed in Corinth and packed in highly artistic small scent jars and shipped in other vessels which sailed west from the port of Lechaion on the shores of the Gulf of Corinth. Lechaion was the second port of Corinth. Contact with the east had its influence on art. The last quarter of the 8th century B.C. saw progressive abandonment of the geometric style in favour of the orientalizing style. Corinthian jars and vases will be now more ornamented with series of exotic birds and animals.

Towards the middle of the 7th century B.C. there was a political change. Kypselos, an ambitious member of the Vahkiades royal family, overthrew the rule of the «one Year Elders» which had succeeded the rule of kings and established himself as a tyrant. He was succeeded by his son Periandros, one of the Seven Sages and he, in turn, by his nephew Psammitichos. Kypselos and Periandros inaugurated a new, brilliant era. Corinth attained the zenith of its power founding the first colonial empire in the world and establishing relations with the rulers of Asia Minor, the East and Egypt. New colonies were founded, Apollonia on the shores of what is now Albania, Potidaea in the Chalkidiki peninsula and a host of smaller ones. Trade flourished, so did the workshops of purple dye and of weavers of fabrics. Ceramics and copperware from Corinth spread the world over. Corinth became the meeting place of mariners, merchants and pleasure seekers. An influx from all over Greece of concubines — among which Laïs, renowned for her beauty — completed the atmosphere of this sinful but most attractive city. The Tyrants became also patrons of art and literature. During this period a new form of poetry called «the dithyramb» was developed at Corinth. It is to Periandros that tradition attributes the bold idea of cutting a canal across the isthmus so that ships could sail from one sea into the other, i.e. from the Saronikos Gulf into the Gulf of Corinth. Technical means at his disposal in those days made the task unfeasible so Periandros resorted to a solution which was practicable. He had built across the isthmus a road laid with thick paving stones. It was called the Diolkos and allowed ships to be mounted on iron cradles on wheels and dragged overland to be launched on the other side. The last of the Kypselides, Psammitichos, was in turn overthrown in 584 B.C. by an oligarchy of merchant noblemen. A fine monument dating back to this period was the ancient temple of Apollo who symbolized order and the aristocratic way of life. Corinth had a lot more to offer to the evolution of architecture. It was Corinthian architects who invented the gable on temples and the familiar Corinthian tiling on temple roofs. It was Kallimachos the Corinthian who, two centuries later, created the Corinthian capital.

The Persian wars at the turn of the 6th to the 5th centuries B.C. spelt the doom of the development of Corinth. Athens built a fleet and overtook Corinth on the world's markets. Piraeus became the great port and the ceramics of Attica became the fashion of the day. New blows were dealt to Corinth by the Peloponnesian War (431-404 B.C.) and the Corinthian War (395-387 B.C.). Corinth buckled under the financial burden and its population thinned out. However, the city picked up again and from 350 to 250 B.C. it became the most important and thickly populated city on the Greek mainland. It was in Corinth that the Greeks, re-united, acclaimed Philip of Macedonia and, later his son Alexander, as generalissimo for the expedition against the Persians. In the following century (3rd century B.C.) Corinth became an active partner in the Achaean League. Collision with Rome became inevitable and at the battle of the Isthmus in 146 B.C. the Roman Lucius Mummius defeated the Greek forces in the last battle which sealed the chapter of Hellenism. The Roman conqueror razed the city to the ground after carrying off its art treasures.

Corinth thus disappeared off the map. Death and desolation reigned supreme for 100 years there where life had flourished. This continued until, unexpectedly, in 44 B.C. thanks to the initiative taken by Julius Caesar and to its unique geographical position, Corinth rose out of its ashes. A new city called Colonia Julia Corinthiensis came into being and was peopled by Italian colonists, Jews and, no doubt by as many of its former inhabitants whose families had contrived to escape death or capture. The new Greco-Roman city attained new prosperity as the seat of the Roman proconsul of the province of Achaïa («Achaïa» being the name used for Greece, Corinth was virtually the new capital of Greece). The large proportion of Jewish inhabitants may have been one of the reasons which prompted Saint Paul, in 51-52 A.D. to visit the city. It was to the Christian community which he founded there that Saint Paul later addressed his famous letters to the Corinthians. In 66-67 A.D. the emperor Nero visited Corinth in order to proclaim the independence of the Greek cities. It was then that he conceived the idea of cutting the canal across the isthmus, using 6,000 slaves captured in Judaea. However, rebellion which broke out in Rome thwarted this plan. Ten years later, an earthquake in Corinth destroyed many of the buildings put up in the days of Augustus Tiberius and Claudius. The city was renovated and endowed with more buildings in a new style by the emperor Hadrian who also built an acqueduct to fetch water from lake Stymphalia. This brilliant initiative was carried on by the Athenian multimilionnaire of his time Herod Atticus.

In subsequent years, Corinth fared less happily. From the 3rd and 4th centuries onward, the city suffered various blows. In 267 A.D. the Herulians ravaged the city. In 375 A.D. another earthquake demolished most of the buildings in the Agora. In 395 A.D. the city was pillaged and burnt by the hordes of Visigotths, under Alaric. More earthquakes caused further damage during the reign of the emperor Justinian. Slav tribes raided Corinth and the rest of the Peloponnese during the 6th and 7th centuries A.D.

This is probably the time when lower Corinth was abandoned, for the first time, by its inhabitants who took refuge up on Acrocorinth. In the 10th century A.D. buildings were again constructed, this time on top of the rubble of the former Agora. The city enjoyed an interval of peace and quiet while being at the same time the seat of the «theme» (meaning district or province, under the Byzantines) of the Byzantine military Governor of the Morea. This held until 1147 when the city was captured and looted by the Normans, who captured Acrocorinth as well. From then on, Acrocorinth changed hands many times. The Greek settlements continued to exist in the coastal plain below. During the centuries of Ottoman rule, a flourishing village developed down in the plain which turned into a town with time. This town was the site of the village presently known as Palaia Korinthos.

TOPOGRAPHICAL MONUMENTS

Traces of the ancient city as it developed into a city-state in ancient times (7th and 6th centuries B.C.) up to the time of its destruction in 146 B.C. have been largely obliterated by subsequent installations and by silting-up. Despite this, it has been possible to identify at several points the walls which enclosed the city on three sides as far as the foot of the Acrocorinth hill which formed the natural bastion of the fourth side. (It is worthy of note that, at certain stages, Corinth was the largest walled city on the Greek mainland, as far as extent is concerned). Two more parallel defensive walls have also been identified as being those which protected the road leading from the city to the port of Lechaion. Two other roads led direct from Corinth to Kechreai, the second port of Corinth and to Sikyon. A notable archaeological discovery was the excavation of the Kerameikos quarter inside the area of the ancient walled town. This was the city potter's district. In the workshops of this district, artisans made, not only the famous — for a period of time — Protocorinthian and Corinthian vases but also large architectural sections for buildings, such as metopes for temples, ornamental tiles for tapering off tiled roofs on building façades, etc. It was only in Corinth, in ancient times, that this particular form of ceramic art was practiced with such zeal. Large clay idols and clay statues were also made. In the northern sector of the town, but inside the city walls, excavations revealed the sanctuary of Asklepios next to the Lerna spring. This was first laid out in the 4th century B.C.

More recent excavations brought to light a sanctuary to Demetra (Ceres) and the Kore of ancient times, just beneath the road leading to Acrocorinth.

The architectural layout of the official centre of the city, with its sanctuaries and public buildings is only partially known and such knowledge does not refer to a period older than the 6th century B.C.

When, in 44 B.C. the Romans rebuilt Corinth as a Greco-Roman city, they buried several of the ravaged buildings in the centre of the ancient city in order to build new ones on top of them. Most of the old buildings, however, were restored and were put back into use, with certain modifications in some cases. These buildings were included in the space where the Romans built their own forum which was also the centre of their city. The ruins of the Roman forum now spread beneath the terrace on which the ancient temple of Apollo stands. Thus, a visit to the archaeological site begins with the ruins of the Roman market place which was laid out mainly in the 1st century A.D. (The buildings in this forum were identified largely thanks to the description made of them by Pausanias who passed through Corinth during one of his tours in the 2nd century A.D.).

From the north, the broad Lechaion Road leads up a gentle gradient to the forum. It is paved with flagstones. Broad, shallow steps at intervals along this road show that it was used for carrying goods up from the port of Lechaion not on wheeled carts but by pack animals. There is a sidewalk on either side. The eastern side of the road is of particular interest for its variety of buildings. To begin with, the visitor can see the Baths of Eurycles, a gift to the city by a Spartan. Further on are the Public Lavatories and beyond them, to the south, a row of Roman Shops. In the space directly behind the shops stretches the Perivolos of Apollo a large, rectangular courtyard enclosed by a colonnade in the Ionian style. When Pausanias passed through Corinth, the centre of the courtyard was dominated by a statue of the god Apollo in bronze. The courtyard, the lavatories and the Perivolos of Apollo took shape in the 1st century A.D. The baths of Eurycles were added in the next century. Excavations beneath the remains of the Roman shops revealed the foundations of an older temple dedicated to the god Apollo, belonging to the 4th century B.C. But this, for reasons unknown, was destroyed a century later.

From here, the visitor will go on to the Fountain of the Lower Peirene. This is a very ancient spring with an abundant flow of water, even in summer. The spring is bound to much legend. The Nymph Peirene, daughter of the river Acheloos, had two sons, Lechaios and Kechrias. On some occasion, the goddess Artemis (Diana) accidentally slew Kechrias. In her grief for the loss of her son, Peirene was transformed into a fountain from which the water, symbolising her tears, flows for ever. According to different legend, Peirene sprang forth with water where Pegasus, the winged horse of Bellerophont, struck his hoof on the ground. The spring was first transformed into a fountain from its natural state in the 7th century B.C. and since then underwent many modifications.

Originally, the water gathered in four tanks carved into the rock and then poured into three cisterns. In front of the cisterns there was a single stone parapet with apertures from which the water could be drawn in jars. Later, the space in front of the parapet was formed into six subterranean cavities behind the façade. The fundamental reformation of the spring took place in the 1st century A.D. and was carried out by the Romans. The Romans built the two-storey façade with arched openings which can be seen to-day. A courtyard was laid out in front and in its midst was the cistern into which the water flowed. The subsequent layout of the courtyard in the shape of a cloveleaf with three massive niches to the north, the west and the east sides, was carried out a century later by the Athenian millionnaire Herod Atticus. Alcoves inside each of the niches housed statues of members of the family of Herod Atticus.

Exactly on a level with the Peirene Fountain, the road from Lechaion ended in front of a marble Triumphal Arch. The arch was built in the 1st century A.D. over the ruins of an older Greek gateway («Propylon») and constituted the entrance to the main market square or forum. Always according to the travel journal of Pausanias, the top of the arch was decorated with two four-horse chariots carrying the Sun God and his son Phaethon. Before this stretches the large space (160 × 95 m.) of the Agora or Roman Forum, surrounded by long and narrow colonnades. In front or behind these were the shops. The space of the Agora was terraced on two levels, north and south with a difference of 4 m between them. The northern section, which was on the lower level, contained the market proper with its shops and arcades. The breastwork, supporting the upper (south) terrace, was built by the Romans and, in front of this what were named the «central shops» were built. In contrast, the remains of the buildings on the upper level showed that they belonged to the administrative centre of the Roman province. Along the northern side of the Agora there was built originally in the 1st century A.D., along the western side the Lechaion road, a large, long and narrow building, the North Basilica. Towards the end of the 2nd century and early in the 3rd century A.D., there was built in front of the Basilica an artistically decorated building in Parian marble which was named the «Captives' Façade». Thus, the Captives' Façade formed the final façade of the Basilica with which it was connected across an open-air courtyard. The lower part of this structure had columns in the Corinthian style while aloft were at least four immense statues representing barbarian prisoners of war. The Basilica which served in all probability as a court of law, had an internal colonnade. In the 3rd century A.D. an additional row of 15 shops were added to the NW side of the Agora and they were called the North-West Shops. These were obscured by an arcade of Corinthian style colonnade. The central shop, now partially restored was later converted into a Christian church (traces of mural paintings in the interior). On the

NW side of the Agora, apart from remains of Roman buildings, there are also several much older Greek buildings. To begin with there are the remains of a large arcade behind the North-West shops, which dated six centuries earlier, which is to say, back to the 3rd century B.C.

The North-West Arcade, as it is called today, appears to have served commercial purposes in the times of the Hellenistic city. In contrast, the apsidal Temple B the Wall with the Triglyphs and the Sacred Fountain were connected with worship and possibly with an oracle which operated in the name of the god Apollo. All three date to the 5th century B.C.

The Wall with the Triglyphs which once upon a time carried tripods and statues, is a low retaining wall, decorated with a triglyph relief cornice. At a certain point in this wall, steps lead to the Sacred Fountain at a level below that of the Agora. The Sacred Fountain, two of whose lionhead copper spouts survive, is, together with the Lower Peirene Fountain and that of Glafke, one of the three oldest fountains in Corinth. It would seem that, in the original lay-out in ancient times, the fountain was in the open air. Later, when the level of the surrounding ground rose, it was converted into a subterranean construction (5th century B.C.). At some stage in the Greek period, it must have run dry with the result that it was filled in and covered up, its existence having remained unknown to the Romans. The Wall with the Triglyphs is also linked by a tunnel (easily traversable by a human being) to the small arched temple to the North. This temple, with an altar at its centre, was probably the site of some minor oracle. The tunnel entrance is concealed by a mobile metope in the retaining wall. This allowed the priests of the temple of Apollo to pass unseen through the tunnel and stand beneath the floor of the altar in the oracle. There, through an invisible peephole they could hear the questions asked by the faithful of their god and the priests could then reply in his name.

Other remains which also date back to the 5th century B.C. are those of the Fish Market, discovered beneath the foundations of the North Basilica (it became named thus on account of the typical construction and layout of its small shops).

Close to this point, a flight of steps leads up to the terrace on which stands the ancient Temple of Apollo. This temple, built in the middle of the 6th century B.C., over the ruins of an older temple, still has seven columns in situ. At one time it was a 38-column (6 × 15) peripteral temple. Internally, it was divided into four parts. On the eastern side a distyle portico in antis led into the main temple or nave. On the western side a replica of the portico at the rear of the temple led into a small chamber (adyton), directly behind the cella where the statue of the god who was worshipped must have stood. Both in the cella and in the adyton, there were internal rows of columns which supported the roof.

The temple is the best existing specimen of the early Doric style and is characteristic for its single columns which are crowned with bulging capitals and for its heavy proportions found only in some of the temples in Sicily The heavy proportions of the columns are offset by the curving of the stylobate, seen for the first time in a Greek temple and brought to its perfection in the Parthenon. At the, northern end of the terrace, a large commercial arcade was built in the 5th century B.C. and to the right of this, a bath. Five centuries later, when the main layout of the Roman Forum was made, the bath and part of the Northern Arcade were demolished to make room for the building of the North Market on the same site. This was a rectangular peristyle court surrounded by shops.

Finishing with the buildings on the terrace of the Temple of Apollo, the way leads back to the square of the Agora. Its eastern side is enclosed by the Julian Basilica, a large rectangular building with an internal colonnade which served as a law courts and was built in the 1st century A.D. It was thus named after the statues of the family of Julius Caesar which were found in it and are now exhibited, together with other Roman antiquities, in the Roman Hall of the Corinth Museum.

At the eastern extremity of the square of the Agora there must have been during the Greek and Hellenistic periods, the track of the ancient city's stadium. Indeed, just in front of the Julian Basilica, at a lower level, traces were found of the starting line-up for the contests. To the south is a curved retaining wall on which probably stood the grandstand of the judges. As no traces of tiers of seats were found in this area, spectators must have squatted on the slopes of the natural mounds formed on either side of the track. Ancient authors have described how, during the Ellotian Games, performed in honour of the Ellotian Athena, races and torch races were held in the Corinth stadium.

On the opposite, western side of the Agora, there are the remains of a row of twelve Roman shops, the Western Shops, as they have been called built behind an arcade. In the middle, the row of shops is interrupted by a broad stairway which leads to the boundary of the Roman temple E of Octavia. Temple E built on a small terrace over the ruins of an older 3rd century B.C. temple, was dedicated to the worship of the imperial family of Augustus. It was built in the 1st century AD. at the same time as the shops and the arcade. At the turn of the 1st century A.D. to the 2nd, six small Roman temples were built on a ledge in front of the arcade of the Western Shops. These temples, of which only the minimum traces remain, were in turn dedicated to Venus-Tyche, Pantheon, Hercules, Neptune, Clarius Apollo and Mercury. The temple of Clarius Apollo was the only one with a north-south orientation. On its eastern side is the elegant Monument of Babbius, with 8 Corinthian columns set on a square base.

At the south side of the square of the Agora, in front of the retaining wall which separates the two terraces, a very large row of shops had been built, known as the Central Shops. These central shops were not set behind any arcade but gave directly onto the market square. At about the middle the row is interrupted by the *Bema* or Rostrum, a rectangular platform with wings extending right and left. From this rostrum, Roman officials addressed the populace in the market square. It must have been in front of this rostrum that Saint Paul must have stood in 51/2 A.D. to face the Roman Consul Gallius (Acts of the Apostles, Chapter 18, Verses 12-18). On this site, at a later date, the Basilica (church) of the Byzantine lower city of Corinth was built. In between the shops, at intervals, are steps which used to lead up to the Upper Agora. The eastern limit of the Upper Agora is marked by the Tabularium (South East Building). This was a building which housed all the public records of the Roman administration. The Tabularium was a rectangular building with an internal colonnade. Its façade carried a colonnade in the Ionian style. The south side of the Upper Agora was enclosed by a very long arcade, more than 150 m in length, the South Stoa (arcade) as it has been named. The South Arcade which was the largest building in ancient Greece was built during the Hellenistic period to counterbalance the Northwest Stoa of comparable design. It had two rows of columns, one external consisting of 71 columns in the Doric style and one internal, consisting of 34 columns in the Ionian style. During excavations along the frontage, several grooves in the groundrock were found which, in all probability had been carved out to permit the fixing of votive offerings looted together with other artistic treasures in the city by the Romans. The layout of the arcade in the Hellenistic period provided for a row of 33 rectangular shops behind the internal row of columns. The shops consisted of a roofed antechamber which communicated with a room behind it. In the rear wall of the room was an exit which probably led out to some provisory latrine. The shops carried a storey above with more rooms. The anterooms in all the shops but two, had a well supplied by water from the Lower Peirene fountain. The abundance of drinking cups found in these

Temple of Apollo
Le Temple d'Apollon
Der Tempel des Apollo

wells led to the interpretation that the row of shops must have been ancient taverns with sleeping quarters in the rooms upstairs. The wells in the anterooms could have served as refrigerators, since the water flowing from the spring could keep the food and wine cool. As the arcade was built, in any case, after the year 350 B.C. which means in the reign of Philip or Alexander, it could have served as a large guest house to provide accommodation for the Greek city representatives, since Corinth, after the battle of Chaeronia in 338 B.C., had become the hub of a Pan-Hellenic Alliance.

The arcade was subsequently subjected to numerous modifications. At the close of the 2nd century A.D. its rear section was basically modified. The shops, for the most part, were demolished to make room for administrative buildings. At the eastern extremity, three Roman buildings were put up. The most westerly was the Office of the Agonothetes, who supervised the Isthmia Athletic Games. The mosaïc floor of the building has survived, showing an athlete wearing a victor's wreath standing before the goddess Eutychia. The next building is the Office of the Roman Governor. It consisted of a vestibule and a room in which there is the base of a statue of a procurator of the Emperor Traïanus. The floor is richly laid with marble paving with coloured veins. The adjoining section of the arcade was converted into a forecourt. The forecourt, through a marble stairway and a portico, leads to the South Basilica, a twin building with the Julian Basilica, and like it once adorned with imperial statues as a kind of stock exchange. Here also statues of Roman emperors were found. To the west of the Basilica there is a most beautiful marble fountain.

At about the centre of the arcade was the beginning of the road which linked the city to the port of Kechreai. This road, as was the case with the roads leading to Sikyon and to Acrocorinth, was paved by the Romans when the Agora was transformed in the 1st century A.D.

To the left of the road stand the remains of the Vouleftirion or Senate. This building, unique for its shape, consists of a façade with two semi-circular apses to right and left. Behind it was a room in the shape of a horseshoe with stone benches inside. Finally, at the western extremity of the arcade there is the ancient road which led to Acrocorinth. This completes the tour of the main Roman Forum. All that is left to be seen are the remains of the Glafki Fountain, Temple C of Akraia Hera, the Theatre and the Odeon, beyond its NW side.

The Glafki Fountain lies 200 m west of the Peirene Fountain and was constructed on the same basic design. The water was transported by ducts to four tanks hewn out of a four-sided rock. The spring is connected by legend with the second wife of Jason, who was the daughter of the King of Corinth. Medea, determined to take revenge upon the faithless Jason, sent a magic gown with her children.
As soon as Glafki wore it, she burst into flames and jumped into the waters of the fountain where she drowned.

The adjoining Roman temple was in all probability dedicated to the goddess Akraia Hera as was the earlier 4th century B.C. temple upon the ruins of which, it was built. The temple was built on the spot where, according to legend, the infuriated Corinthians stoned the children of Medea. A colonnade surrounds the temple with an opening in the middle of its eastern side. This was the point at which the ancient road to Sikyon began.

A little further North are the Theatre and the Odeon. The Theatre, first built in the 5th century B.C., could seat 15,000 It was modified, however, on several occasions and in the early part of the 3rd century A.D., the orchestra pit was modified and fitted with a duct which could bring water in so that scenes of naval battles could be enacted. An inscription found on this spot gave the story of Androcles and the lion.

In contrast, the Odeon is Roman having been built in the 1st century A.D.

It seated 3,000 and was intended for the conduct of musical contests. After a fire which destroyed its interior, it was converted into a gladiators arena. In the second century A.D. the Odeon was linked to the Theatre by a court, presented by Herod Atticus. In a space west of the Theatre and the Odeon, excavations revealed, apart from the Potter's Quarter, the remains of a fine Roman villa with beautiful mosaïcs which can be seen in the Museum. The space East of the Odeon and the Theatre has not yet been excavated. Here, according to Pausanias, stood the very ancient sanctuary of Halinitis Athena. East of the Roman Forum, excavations uncovered a Roman amphitheatre which was intended for duels between gladiators and for fights with wild animals.

ACROCORINTH

The impressive walls of the fortress which are among some of the most beautiful in Greece, are linked to the fortunes of the Byzantine and post-Byzantine city of Corinth. Of the older fortifications of Greek days, only one section has survived which served basically as a foundation for the walls which are visible today. The main fortification must have been carried out in the 10th century A.D. at the time when Corinth was again prospering as capital of the Byzantine province of the Morea. It was from then on that the citadel changed hands among a string of conquerors who claimed the region and left their stamp on the walls. The Normans in the 12th century were followed by the Franks of the 4th Crusade who, after many adventures lost it back to the Byzantines for a brief period. These, in 1458, were followed by the Turks from whom the Venetians snatched it in 1687 only to lose it again to the Turks in 1715. Acrocorinth became Greek again in 1822.

In order to attain the summit of the fortress one has first to traverse a defensive line consisting of three consecutive portals, one outer, one intermediary and one inner. These were interconnected with inclined ramps. The outer portal was defended by a moat over which there was a drawbridge. On the top, the interior of the fortress is a jumble of remains of various buildings which span four centuries from the 14th to the 18th. Walls of houses and Byzantine churches mingle with ruins of Venetian towers and Turkish mosques.

Remains of antique times have disappeared completely under the structures of later times. In those times, the whole Acrocorinthos rock was dedicated to the worship of the Armed Aphrodite where a thousand courtesans were said to offer religious prostitution.

This temple dedicated to the goddess of Syrian origin, Aphrodite-Astarte was built on the highest point of the rock. From this point, on a clear day, there is a panoramic view which makes even the Parthenon visible. To the south is the ancient spring of Upper Peirene which is the spot where, according to legend, Bellerophont caught Pegasus. To the SW of Acrocorinth, Penteskoufi, another Frankish castle, was built between the years 1205-1210.

Agora and sacred spring
L'Agora et la Fontaine sacrée
Agora und Heilige Quelle

Lechaion Road and the Acrocorinth
Rue de Léchaion et l'Acrocorinthe
Lechaionstraße und Akrokorinth

Bema
Béma
Bema

Fountain of Peirene
Fontaine Pirène
Peirene-Quelle

ACROCORINTH : Gate of the fortress ▲
AÇROCORINTHE : Entrée de la forteresse
AKROKORINTH : Eingang zur Festung

Roman Temple
Temple Romain
▼ Römischer Tempel

THE MUSEUM OF ANCIENT CORINTH

Excavations carried out all over the province of Corinthia since 1896, are the work of the American School of Classical Studies and of the Greek Archaeological Society. All finds which were movable are now housed in the Museum of ancient Corinth.

In the pre-historic gallery of the museum, weapons, tools, vases, ornaments and various art miniatures belonging to the Neolithic Age and the Bronze Age are exhibited. These come mainly from the regions of Nemea, Zygouries and pre-historic settlements which existed in the vicinity of the Isthmus. A special class of the pottery on display is what is known as «Ephyraïka» which is made of the easily distinguishable pale Corinthian clay, decorated with elegant patterns, belonging to the Mycenaean period.

The exhibits in the galleries containing Greek antiquities come from the area of ancient Corinth and from its formal sanctuary at Isthmia. The collection is dominated by ceramics of ancient Corinth, mostly vases which cover an entire millenium B.C. and range from Protogeometric to Geometric, Protocorinthian, Corinthian and vases made in imitation of the red and black figured style of Attic pottery and, finally, pottery of the late Greek era up to the time of the Roman conquest. It was with the Protocorinthian vases (725-625 B.C.) in which the black decorative style was first launched, that Corinth dominated the Mediterranean markets for a whole century. The most frequent shapes are the alabasters and minute aryballoi with a thick narrow neck to impede too easy flow of the precious content (perfumes). It is on 8th century B.C. Corinthian vases that some of the oldest inscriptions in Greek have been found. Apart from clay vases and figurines, the Corinthian potters also made small, painted, clay altars. Among sculpture belonging to the Archaic period are a sphinx of limestone and the ancient marble stoup from the temple of Poseidon at Isthmia. There are also some copper exhibits, among which a Corinthian type helmet.

In the next gallery there are statues mainly of the Hellenistic and Roman times but also some Byzantine and post-Byzantine pottery, crockery, coins and minor objects. There are also three mosaïc floors which originate from a Roman villa excavated near the Keramikos (pottery quarter). There is a fine 4th century A.D. head of a statue from the very complete series of Roman statuary (members of the families of Augustus, Antonine the Pious, Caracalla etc.) outstanding among which is the fine head of Nero Julius Caesar, son of Germanicus. There are also Roman copies of classical heads such as that of Sappho (probably by Silanion), the Doryphoros of Polykleitos, Tyche, Artemis, Dionysos (maybe by Praxiteles) etc., also a neo-Attic relief of the dancing Maenads. In addition, there are sculptured fragments of buildings.

In the Museum vestibule there is one of the oldest known Greek mosaïcs (approximately 400 B.C.) which depicts two griffins attacking a horse and in the same room is a head of the city's benefactor Herod Atticus. In a special gallery there are finds from the Asclepeion. Finally, in the inner court of the Museum, various reliefs from the Theatre are exhibited, as well as various decorative Byzantine reliefs.

Terracotta statuette of a seated woman; Archaic era.
Statuette corinthienne en terre cuite d'une femme assise, époque archaïque
Kleine Terrakotta-Figur

Roman cup of a very rare kind with relief decoration, 1st cent. A.D.
Vase Romain de type rare avec décoration en relief (1er s. après J.-C.)
Schwarzbemalter Tonbecher

Fragment of a decorated Corinthian altar of the 6th cent. B.C.
On the left side, a lion. On the right, a fight between a pygmy and a crane

Partie d'un autel corinthien en terre cuite avec représentations.
A gauche : d'un lion, à droite : de la scéne d'une bataille entre cicognes et pygmées (VIème s. av. J.-C.)

Geometric Vase
Vase de style géométrique
Geometrische Vase

Attic black-figured Cylix
Cylix Attique à figures noires ▶
Attische schwarzfigurige Kylix

Attic red-fiigured Vase
Vase Attique à figures rouges
Attische rotfigurige Vase

Attic red-figured plate
Plat attique à figures rouges ▶
Attischer rot figuriger Teller

Mosaics from the Roman Villa
Mosaïques de la villa Romaine
Fußbodenmosaiken aus der römischen Villa

Head of Fortuna (Tyche)
Tête de Tyché (Fortune)
Kopf der Tyche (Fortuna)

Little idol Byzantine. Terracotta head.
Idole Byzantine. Tête de Terre cuite.

MYCENAE

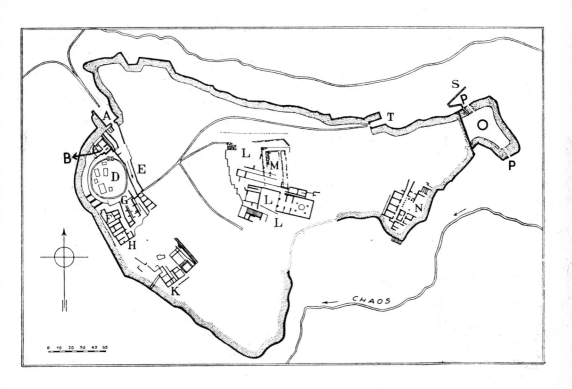

PLAN OF MYCENAE
A. Lion Gate — **B.** Granary — **D.** Grave Circle A — **E.** Great Ramp — **F, G, H, K.** Buildings
of the Lower Acropolis — **L.** Royal Palace — **M.** Hellenistic Temple — **N.** House of Columns —
O. North Eastern Extension — **P.** Tunpels — **S.** Subterranean Fountain — **T.** Northern Gate.

Introduction : Once upon a time, ages and ages ago, Danaos, twin brother
of Aegyptos, quarreled with his brother on the quesiton of who should reign over
Egypt. He found himself obliged to go into exile with his fifty daughters — the
Danaïdes — and one day landed on the shores of the waterless Argos where he
became king. Thanks to Danaos and to his daughter Amymone, Argos acquired
the spring which goes under her name and became a fertile area. When Amymone
married Poseidon, ruler of the seas, Nauplios who later founded the city of
Nauplion was born.

Danaë was the great granddaughter of Danaos and when Jupiter passed as a golden rain through her body, she gave birth to Perseus. When he grew up, he decapitated the terrible Medusa and set Andromeda free who then became his wife. After this, he founded the city of Mycenae where the famous family of the Atreidae reigned. In Tyrins, Eurystheus was king and it was he who ordered his cousin Hercules to strangle the fierce lion which lived in a cave near Nemea. Hercules also slew the dreaded watermonster Hydra which laid waste the Lerna district.

From Danaos, all Greeks were known as Danaoi. So, according to legend, Argolis appears as the cradle of the Greek nation and Danaos as the father of their tribe. In actual fact, the fertile Argive plain had been inhabited since eight thousand years ago. However, the first known pre-historic settlements such as Lerna, Argos, Prosymna, Midea, Mycenae, Tiryns, etc. did not appear until 5.000 years later marked the Early Helladic era (2800 to 2000 B.C.). Life rolled on, evolving somewhat slowly at first but soon gathered momentum, after the first known Greek-speaking tribes migrated (2100 B.C.) into the area, peacefully in some cases or forcefully in others. The new inhabitants spoke an archaïc form of Greek and showed all the characteristic intellectual traits of the Greek race. Their arrival gave birth to a new era known as the Mid-Helladic (2000 to 1600 B.C.). Within less than five hundred years, the first significant Helladic civilization grew up centred upon Mycenae. Mycenae which was first known after the excavations of the pioneer Heinrich Schliemann gave its name to the next era (1600 or 1580 to 1100 B.C.) which became known as the Mycenaean era. The Mycenaean civilization stemming from the royal palaces with their fabulous art and Linear B Script was the immediate forerunner of ancient Greek civilization.

MYCENAE AND THE MYCENAEAN CIVILIZATION

Early in the 16th century B.C., the Mycenaean settlement spread along the slopes of the Acropolis of Mycenae and in the surrounding area. The summit of the Acropolis was, without doubt, the site of a palace whose traces were obliterated by subsequent palace buildings. There was also a simple enclosure for the compound. The palace was inhabited by the ruling dynasty the members of whose family were buried with every pomp and circumstance in the deep graves of the mid-helladic burial ground which stretched along the western slope of the hill. Later, surrounding the royal tombs Grave Circles A and B were built. In the royal tombs of the two Circular Graves there were seen for the first time large quantities of gold objects which were buried with the dead and also burial rites unknown, until then, in the helladic area. Such rites were connected with worship of the dead and belief in a form of existence after death and judgement of souls. The abundance of gold and the foreign origin of the burial rites led to the theory that the Achaeans brought the gold and the new ideas from Egypt where they had served as mercenaries to the Pharaos of the XVIIIth Dynasty. To be more precise, the Achaeans had been enlisted by the Pharaos in their attempt to rid the valley of the Nile of the invading Hyksos tribes.

The Minoan and Cycladic appearance of the ornaments in the royal tombs bear witness to the fact that the Achaeans were familiar with the Minoan civilization. It would seem, therefore, that trade and continuous intensification of contact with the peoples of the Aegean Sea brought the Achaeans, from early times, into contact with the amazing achievements of the Minoans. The sturdy warrior, dazzled by the outward magnificence and finesse of Minoan civilization, inevitably began to imitate not only the Minoan way of life but also its art. During the last decades of the 16th century B.C., the shaft graves were abandoned and impressive, vaulted tombs began to be used for royalty. In the years which followed, contact with the Minoan civilization became more substantial and Cretan elements became grafted onto the body of Mycenaean civilization.

It was at this period that Mycenaean power began to assert itself, at the expense, of course, of the Minoans who had been all-powerful until then. Perhaps a contributory factor towards this switch came from the eruption of the volcano on the island of Santorin, towards the close of the 16th century B.C., resulting in the destruction of several Cretan positions. Around the year 1450 B.C. came the final terrible eruption of the same volcano. Knossos and the principal Minoan centres were laid waste by the earthquakes and tidal waves which swept the shores of Crete. Amid the general panic and turmoil, Achaeans (Mycenaeans)) from the Peloponnese invaded Crete and set up at Knossos a new Achaean-Mycenaean dynasty. Shortly after 1400 B.C., the Knossos palace buildings were finally gutted by fire. Mycenaean expansion had become complete. Unchallenged by any serious rival, Mycenaean trade spread as far as the Lipari islands of Sicily but, above all, dominated the shores of Syria, Palestine, Asia Minor and Egypt. Mycenae became the powerful centre of Greece. Cultural achievements of the Mycenaean civilization spread to every corner of the known helladic world. A uniform civilization took shape not only throughout mainland Greece and in the Aegean but also in the Eastern Mediterranean. Shortly after 1350 B.C., the first cyclopean walls were built around Mycenae and elsewhere. The first monumental type of palaces were built inside them. It is mainly from the palaces of the various Mycenaean centres that most of the terracotta plaques have been found with inscriptions in Linear B script, thus named because it developed from the Minoan Linear A Script, after the Mycenaeans occupied Knossos. The deciphering of this script by Michael Ventris showed that the Mycenaeans spoke a Greek dialect. Linear B Script is the first known form of the Greek language.

About 100 years later (that is to say, around 1250 B.C.), the West wall was built at Mycenae which doubled the area of the Acropolis and enclosed Circular Grave A inside the walled compound. Thus secure from possible pillage, the burial enclosure became a place of worship. At this point, an impressive, fortified gateway was built, the Lions Gate. Another, known as the Northern Gate, was built into the northern side of the walls.

Sometime about the year 1240 B.C. the palace at Mycenae suffered damage but was rebuilt larger and more impressive. Shortly before the close of the 13th century B.C., the N.E. extension was added to the defensive walls which took in the underground spring which rendered the Acropolis larger and self-sufficient in water.

Homer's epic poem places the campaign of the Achaeans against Troy in the time of the generation of the 13th century B.C. Excavations carried out on the site of pre-historic Troy by Heinrich Schliemann, proved that the Trojan War was no myth.

It appears that, around 1200 B.C., the Achaeans engaged in an expedition to the Asia Minor shores which lasted several years. Expeditionary forces from the whole of Mycenaean Greece took part in this operation, under the leadership, according to tradition, of the Mycenaean king Agamemnon. Although the expedition set off with intention of settling Achaeans in Asia Minor, it ended up with the plundering of certain cities only. One of the incidents in this campaign — probably the most important — was the siege and capture of Troy, sung with feeling by contemporary and subsequent poets. In the four centuries which followed, the ballads formed a great epic cycle with the Iliad as its mainstay. The final shaping of the Iliad took place in Ionia in the 8th century B.C. and is attributed to Homer. In the years which followed the Trojan War, political equilibrium in the East was upset by raids carried out by the «People of the Sea», as recorded in Egyptian sources. These seaborne raiders literally stormed and swept away the empire of the Hittites in the interior of Asia Minor, leaving behind them a trail of ruins and ashes. Destruction of the coastal areas of Asia Minor, Syria and Palestine dealt a mortal blow to Mycenaean trade with the cities of the East and caused the decay of the Mycenaean palaces whose power derived from overseas dealings. A wave of emigration to the Near East swept across mainland Greece.

Towards the middle of the 12th century B.C. the Mycenaean world already in the process of gradual disintegration, received the coup de grâce from the descent of the Dorians from the North. The large Mycenaean centres were finally destroyed. At Mycenae the walls were left standing and the area continued to be inhabited. In the Persian wars, a small contingent of Mycenaeans fought alongside other Greeks at the battles of Thermopylae and Plataiae. In 468 B.C., however, the Argives captured and destroyed the Acropolis.

Two centuries later, they repaired the walls and formed a small town which filled the area inside and outside the walls and this town survived until Roman times. The last mention of Mycenae was made by Pausanias who passed through Mycenae toward the middle of the 2nd century A.D. and saw its walls, the Lions Gate, the Perseia Fountain, etc.

EXCAVATIONS

The first systematic excavations were undertaken by Heinrich Schliemann in 1874-1876 and later by the Greek archaeologist G. Stamatakis. Later still, the initiative was assumed by the Greek Archaeological Society under Tsountas. Early in the 20th century, the British School of Archaeology carried out extensive excavations under the supervision of Professor Wace. His work was completed by Lord W. Taylour. In recent years archaeological research has been resumed by the Greek Archaeological Society and the task has been entrusted to Professor G. Mylonas.

MYCENAEAN MYTHOLOGY

The legendary founder of Mycenae was Perseus. However, the hero whose name became associated with Homer's «golden» Mycenae and the Trojan War was that of Agamemnon. Thanks to Agamemnon and the disasters which befell his family, the name of Mycenae survived throughout the whole of the subsequent Greek period and Mycenae passed into the sphere of eternity.

The two heroes belong to two different families. One was Perseid and the other an Atreidae. Both families, however, had one characteristic in common, their founders Danaos and Pelops were both of Eastern origin.

According to tradition, Perseus founded Mycenae and the city walls by using the legendary Cyclopes who had previously built the walls of Tiryns. The writers of these legends indicate that the event took place somewhere in the first half of the 14th century B.C. (1400 to 1350 B.C.). Pausanias maintained that Perseus named his city Mycenae either from the fact that the rivet which held the blade of his sword in the handle («Mykis» in Greek) fell off in that region, which he took to be a favourable omen, or because when he stooped to pull out a mushroom (also «Mykis» in Greek) to slake his thirst he found underneath it a rich natural spring (the Perseian Fountain). The descendants of Perseus reigned at Mycenae for at least three generations. The last member of this dynasty was Eurystheus, the king who caused his cousin Hercules to undertake his famous tasks. Eurystheus was killed in battle in Attica during an expedition against the descendants of Hercules and against the Athenians. As he left no heir, the Mycenaeans acclaimed Atreus, son of Pelops as their king, who had taken refuge in the royal court of Eurystheus. However, rivalry between Atreus and his brother Thyestes over the throne of Mycenae and the love affair between Thyestes and the wife of Atreus, ended in the abominable «Thyestian Dinner» at which Atreus entertained his brother to a banquet at which unknown to the latter he had served up meat from the flesh of the children of Thyestes. The curse which Thyestes later cast upon Atreus for the ghastly deed fell not upon Atreus but upon his descendants. Always according to tradition, Agamemnon succeeded Atreus on the throne of Mycenae around the year 1220 B.C. while his brother Menelaos reigned in Sparta. Paris eloped with Helen, wife of Menelaos and this triggered off the Trojan War. Agamemnon was elected generalissimo of the expeditionary force organized against Troy by all the Greek city states but, in order to get the fleet under way, Agamemnon had to sacrifice his daughter Iphigenia.

Ten years later, Clytaimnestra, Agamemnon's wife took revenge for the death of Iphigeneia. After the destruction of Troy, Agamemnon returned to Mycenae and there, with the help of her lover Aegisthos, Agamemnon was murdered by his wife. (According to Eratosthenis, Troy was destroyed in 1184 B.C.). Eight years later, Orestis, son of Agamemnon, killed his mother and her lover. A short while later, Mycenae was destroyed by the Dorians, according to legend.

THE ACROPOLIS OF MYCENAE

The Acropolis of Mycenae is located at the N.E. extremity of the valley of Argos and dominates the only pass which links the province of Argolis to that of Corinth, now known as the «Dervenakia Pass». The Acropolis is built on a triangular hill which stands about 40 m. above the surrounding land. On the southern side, a deep gorge known as «Havos» (possibly derived from the word «Chaos») separates the hill of Mycenae from the precipitous hill of Sara. On the northern side Mycenae is flanked by the hill of the prophet Eli.

Fortification : The city walls have two gates. The main gate on the N.W. corner was known as the Lions Gate while a secondary gate was let into the northern side. The former was the terminal of the main approach road while the latter served traffic from the hinterland. At the N.E. extremity of the fortifications there were two small auxiliary exits. The fortified enclosure is an area of 30,000 m². The walls were built in three stages. Midway through the 14th century B.C. the old compound was built its northern wall and part of its S.E. wall having survived. About a century later (1250 B.C. approximately) the western wall and the Lion Gate were built, which about doubled the area of the Acropolis and took in the Circular Grave A . Immediately after this, the northern gate was built. Finally, around 1200 B.C., the N.E. extension was built and this took in the subterranean spring, the Acropolis having assumed its final shape, as seen in the present day.

The walls follow the natural contour of the rock and are 5 to 8 m. thick. They do not stand at their original height which has been estimated at 12 m. They have survived in their entirety except for a small section on the southern side where the wall fell into the Havos gorge carrying with it the S.E. corner of the palace building.

The walls were built in the «cyclopean» manner, that is to say, with large, irregular, unhewn boulders, set without any specific system. Spaces between them were filled with smaller stones or with earth or clay. An exception to this form of building exists in the western side of the tower of the Lion Gate, at a point in the western walls known as the Polygonal Tower and part of the façade of the N.E. extension. These sections were repaired in the hellenistic era in the familar «polygonal» manner.

In the vicinity of the gates, construction has been carried out with greater care. The two gates, with their towers and adjoining walls are built in the manner known in Greek as «pseudoïsodomic» which, in fact implies boulders which have been squared with hammer and saw and have been set in horizontal rows.

The particularly large size of the boulders used caused people in subsequent ages to relate them to giant beings, the Cyclopes, who were considered as the only living creatures able to handle them. It was from the Cyclopes that this form of building got its name «Cyclopean». The whole appearance of the Acropolis must have been impressive. If one pauses to reflect that in Mycenaean times there were neither guns nor siege machines and that the only weapons were a few portable bows and arrows, swords and lances, it becomes obvious that an Acropolis of this construction could only succumb as the result of treason or of starvation.

The Lion Gate : The approach to the main gate resembles a ramp which forms a kind of small, open-air courtyard in front of the gate. On the eastern flank of the courtyard rises the wall of the Acropolis while the western flank is dominated by a tower which juts out of the wall. The occupants of the tower could shoot arrows into the unprotected right flank of an attacking force because shields were held by the left arm and protected that side of the warrior. The Lion Gate is an astounding monument of heavy stonework and shows the genius of the architect. It consists of four monolithic blocks of immense dimensions, one forming the threshold, two converging pilasters and the top slab holding them in position. The threshold and the slab forming the top of the gate each weigh more than 20 tons. The opening of the gate was about three metres high and as wide. The gate itself consisted of a two-leaf door of wood and ornamented with copper strips. Each leaf was nailed onto a wooden beam whose lower and upper ends fitted into sockets hewn out of the threshold and the upper slab or lintel. The doors could swing inwards only.

To prevent the doors swinging outwards, the façade of the pilasters was so carved as to provide a frame. When the Mycenaeans wished to close the gate from within, they placed in position a horizontal beam whose ends fitted into a square niche carved into the side of each pilaster at about the height of the eyes of an average man. Each pilaster also had one eliptical cavity into which it would seem that the handles of the doors fitted when they were wide open and flattened against the pilasters.

The surface of the threshold was deliberately kept rough obviously in order to spare pack animals the risk of slipping as they went through. There are also three grooves cut across the threshold and served to provide an outlet for rainwater when the gates were closed. The lintel over the pilasters is thicker at its centre, a precaution taken to counter any possibility of its giving way under the weight of the heavy superstructure. Over this slab covering the gate there has been left a relieving triangle built in a corbelling out manner. Thanks to this triangle, the covering slab is spared much of the weight of the superstructure which is transferred in this manner from the edges of the slab to the pilasters and the threshold. The triangular opening is filled in with a plaque with lions carved onto it. It was this which gave the gate its name. The lions are presented facing one another with their front paws resting on two small, united altars on which rests the pillar. The upper part of the pillar holds part of a wooden superstructure (entablature). The heads of the lions have been lost. There can be little doubt that they had been carved out of some other materials and were turned towards the onlooker. The entire combination formed a sort of coat of arms of the royal house of Mycenae. The lions may even have had an additional deterent meaning, symbolising protection of the royal heraldry and driving danger away. The whole presentation may have had the meaning of a massive amulet. Although, in Europe, there are more ancient examples of sculpture, the Lion Gate of Mycenae is looked upon as the first and oldest example.

Inner Court — Building of the Granary. Just inside the Lion Gate there is a small, square courtyard which was once roofed. In the left-hand wall of the courtyard and only a little above ground, a non-symmetrical niche has been left between wall and rock. In all probability the shrine of some deity fitted into this niche which was designed to house the deity which helped to guard the city gate.

In the space behind the right-hand side of the courtyard, a stairway led up to the ramparts and the turret fortress. To the west of the stairway are the remains of a building which leaned upon the cyclopean walls. Apart from its basement, this building must have been at least two storeys high. Charred grain was found in clay jars. This discovery caused the space to be referred to as the granary. It is far more likely, however, that it served as the billets for the guardroom staff who maintained their rations in the basement of their building. The granary was destroyed by fire in about 1120 B.C. at the same time as the other buidlings on the Acropolis were gutted.

Grave Circle A . South of the Granary lies Grave Circle A which, around the year 1250 B.C. enclosed the royal section of the mid-Helladic burial ground which stretched down the hillside. It consists of a circular space of 28 m. diameter surrounded by two rows of upright stone slabs which were covered or roofed by similar slabs. The strip of ground, about a metre wide, between the two rows of

The lion gate
La Porte des lions
Das Löwentor

▲ The Royal Grave Circle A
Le Cercle Royal A
Das Rund der Königlichen Gräber A   **Grave Circle A** (reconstruction). ▼

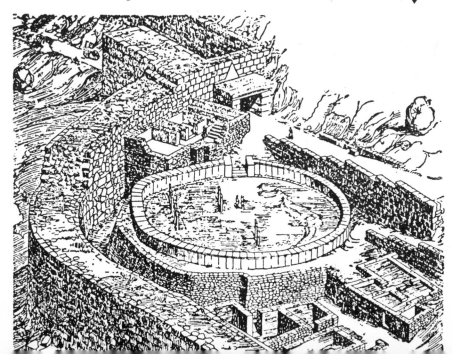

upright slabs, was filled in with stones and earth. Thus a breastwork was formed all round the space, varying in height from one to one and a half metres, according to the westward slope of the land. Access to the Circle was in the northern side, opposite the Lions Gate and consisted of a threshold and pilasters built in the same manner as the Grave Circle itself.

Excavations in the western section of the Circle unearthed six royal shaft graves usually quoted in Latin figures I to IV. These tombs differed in size and depth and appeared to have been used for several burials because a total of 19 skeletons were found in the three of them, belonging to men, women and children. The inner sides of the tombs were lined in dry, low, stone walls on which rested the end of horizontal wooden beams which supported the roofs of the tombs. The roof on each tomb was made of boughs amd slate tiles. Onto the roof of each tomb, which was well below ground level, they threw earth until it came flush with the ground level. They then piled more earth on top, forming a small mound which was crowned with a tombstone. These tombstones are now to be seen in the Athens Archaeological Museum. Some of them show, either engraved or in relief, hunting scenes or chariot racing or carry simple decorative lines. They are the oldest examples of large scale sculpture in Greece.

Schliemann, who in 1876 discovered and excavated Grave Circle A, found in the tombs a treasure of gold and other ornaments which were buried with the dead. In certain cases, the faces of the men were covered with gold masks while the garments of the women must have had numerous gold ornaments sewn on to them judging by the number which were found scattered around. There were even some gold diadems, combs, earrings and scales for weighing the soul. It is estimated that the gold objects thus unearthed weighed a total of some 14 kilos. Among other discoveries were some excellent samples of Mycenaean craftsmanship such as inlaid daggers and swords and jars for pouring out libations made in the shape of a head or a whole animal. All these finds are exhibited in the Mycenaean Hall of the Athens National Archaeological Museum. Schliemann believed that Agamemnon and his family had been buried in Grave Circle A but Agamemnon must have reigned at the turn of the 13th to the 12th century B.C. These graves date back about four centuries earlier and belong to the royal family of Mycenae of the 16th century B.C. which was given the name of the Dynasty of the Shaft Graves.

Houses of the Lower Acropolis. South of the Grave Circle «A», on the slope of the rock. a whole row of buildings has been excavated, which stretched along the west wall with only a narrow passage separating them from it. Their foundations are built in sturdy stone masonry. The portion of each building above ground was completed in unbaked brick which supported a wooden roof. Some of the buildings had a storey built either above a basement or a ground floor habitation. As a rule, basements were used for storage while living quarters were above. There are two building complexes. The first comprises three typical Mycenaean houses with storage space and living quarters and were given the names of the House of the Warrior Vase, the Ramp House and the South House. The first got its name because of the discovery of a Mycenaean vase showing warriors and the second because it is built alongside a small ramp. The second comprises the two, official sanctuaries of Mycenae and the mansion known as the Tsountas House. The eastern sanctuary was described by its excavator as a Temple while the one to the west was called the Building of the Murals.

The interior of the temple which was dedicated to the worship of infernal gods and demons, was found to contain a large number of clay effigies of human or monstrous shapes and coiled snakes. These idols with a circular, hollow body and disproportionately small hands, raised in some form of supplication, were apparently set upon staves and paraded round, as happens with banners during litanies. The monstrous appearance of the idols supports the view that they may represent the Furies. The interior of the House of the Murals has showed sections of wall painting. The figure of a goddess clasping sheaves of wheat or branches gave reason to suppose that it signified the goddess of vegetation or fertility.

The Tsountas House, further south, consists of three sections : a row of store-rooms near the city wall, a mansion towards the higher ground to the east with a built-in hearth in the centre and an adjoining sanctuary with a low, built-in hearth. A small tablet found in the interior of the sanctuary showed a warrior goddess and this lent weight to the assumption that the sanctuary itself was dedicated to some goddess of war, possibly a forerunner of the goddess Athena. In front of the façade of the sanctuary, there are the remains of a low altar. The altar stands at the head of a broad approach road of good construction which descends the slope of the acropolis. This seems once to have been a roofed ceremonial approach to the sanctuaries which had murals on the walls on either side and led the Mycenaeans to their formal places of worship.

The Large Ramp. The Royal Road climbed by a majestic ramp from the court-yard of the Lion Gate to the Mycenaean palace on the summit. The road, following the line of fortification, climbs first to the S.E. with a width of about 5.00-5.50 m. It then swings to the north and N.W. and continued as a broad road. From the southern end of the climb, there is a full view of the Graves Enceinte, the houses of the Lower Acropolis and the western wall (at which point began the road leading to the Lower Acropolis, obliterated by the foundations of an oil press built later in the Hellenistic era). The continuation of the road to the N.E. has not survived but appears to have forked. The left fork apparently led to the N.W. palace entrance while the right fork led to the large S.W. stairway of the palace. The present path leads directly to the N.W. palace entrance.

The Palace. The Mycenaean Palace is a grouping of buildings set on two levels. Very few ramains of the buildings of the upper level survive. The lower level stretched down the S.W. side of the hill. The Palace main entrance was at the N.W. corner. There was a four-sided Propylon or porch with an inner and outer colonnade with single row of columns (bases and foundations visible). In front of the outer colonnade, there was a small, cobbled courtyard. There is another courtyard in front of the inner colonnade of the Propylon. It is from this point that the long west corridor began, leading to the western main palace entrance. Only its threshold has survived. At the N.W. corner of the long corridor a staircase leads to the northern corridor and to the apartments of the summit of the hill.

The large western entrance was the main entrance for all parts of the palace. On the northern side of the main entrance was an anteroom probably used as an office. From this main entrance also began the southern corridor which, in the first constructional stage of the palace, led to the apartments on the upper level.

However, in later Mycenaean years, its eastern extremity was blocked by a wall. A smaller corridor to the S.E. led to the Great Court. This Great Court and the buildings surrounding it was the most important section of the palace and, fortunately, is the best preserved section. It is here that the Mycenaean ruler received his official guests, it was here that the hall where audiences were held existed, the hall for ceremonies and official banquets and the guestroom. The Great Court was open air its dimensions being 15 × 12 m with the view to the south unrestricted. The flooring was of hard material overlaid with lime mortar, marked out in squares with some form of painted ornamentation which has not survived. The eastern side of the Great Court was flanked by the main palace building 23 m long by 11.5 m wide. The hall was a colonnade giving on to the Great Court with two wooden pillars which carried the roof. The pillars were burnt but their stone pedestals have survived. The anteroom was of the same shape and size as the hall to which it was connected by a single-leaf door (whose threshold survives).

The walls of the anteroom were decorated with frescoes, sections of which are now exhibited in the National Archaeological Museum. The floor was framed in gypsum flagstones while the rest was laid in lime mortar with paintings on it. The eastern side of the anteroom or vestibule had an opening which closed not with a door but without doubt with a curtain or screen and led to the «domos», a room 13 m × 11.5 m which was impressive for its size. In the centre was a circular hearth 3.40 m in diameter. The hearth was ringed by a rim of porous stone decorated with painted shapes in black, red and white. Four wooden columns round the hearth supported a protruding aperture in the roof, through which the smoke escaped. This room likewise had mural decoration and its floor was made in a manner similar to that of the vestibule. This must have been the king's throne room, though no throne has survived (as with other Mycenaean palaces). The throne itself was probably located half way along the south wall. On the west flank of the Great Court stood the guestroom with its bath. There are the remains of an almost square room with a small open-air courtyard giving off its southern side. The interior of this room was decorated with frescoes and there was a rectangular hearth in the middle of its northern wall. There is nothing left of a smaller room to the west. The large staircase of the S.W. palace entrance led to the courtyard of the guestroom. Only a few steps of this large staircase have survived. During the final constructional phase of the palace complex, when the southern corridor was blocked with a wall, a door was let into the northern side of the reception hall and thence a wooden staircase led to the apartments of the upper level. A long and narrow anteroom has survived here which had low benches along its walls and a rectangular hearth. From its mural decorations which resembled embroidered curtains, it was called the Anteroom of the Curtains. East of this was the staircase which led to the rooms of the upper level. Very few remains of these have survived. The most noteworthy is the corner of a room with its floor painted red and two low benches along its walls, commonly referred to as the Red Bath after the legend of the assassination

The Mycenaean Acropolis
◄ L'Acropole de Mycènes
Die Mykenische Akropolis

The Postern Gate to the north
La Poterne du Nord
Das Nord-Tor   ▼

of Agamemnon whereas, in actual fact, this was never a bathroom. Mycenaean structures on the crest of the hill were destroyed when a temple was built there in the 7th century B.C., probably dedicated to the goddess Athena. During the Hellenistic era a second and larger temple was built there. This second temple, of which the embankment and the foundations of the outer wall have survived, was a rectangular structure of rare orientation for a Greek temple, that is to say it had been built on a north to south axis. Nothing is left of the buildings which stood on the eastern slope of the hill where the private quarters of the royal family were sited, the women's apartments, the bedrooms, servants quarters, etc.

Buildings of the Eastern Side : Excavations on the eastern slope of the Acropolis revealed four buildings to which the names of Artists' Workshop, House of Columns, Building C and Building D were given. The first two form part of the eastern palace wing. The Artists' Workshop was the place where artists and artisans lived and worked for account of the Mycenaean ruler. It consists of a long and narrow central courtyard alongside which run two narrow corridors. The west corridor leads into four or more rooms and the eastern corridor likewise leads to four rooms which had a second storey. Access to the building was from the northern side and gave on to a narrow horizontal corridor which gave on to the other corridors and to the rooms on the eastern side. The partition wall on which rested the four eastern rooms of the Artists' Workshop formed the western wall of a long corridor which led from the entrance to the central courtyard of the House of Columns. The bases which have survived showed that the courtyard was surrounded by columns. Its eastern side gave on to the Little Palace, as it was known. Parallel with this the foundations have survived of the staircase which led to the second storey. Along the western side of the courtyard there are the remains of the corridors which led to the basement or cellars.

North Eastern Extension : The N.E. extension to the fortifications was made in about 1200 B.C. This extension was undertaken in order to render the Acropolis self-sufficient as regards water by the construction of a water reservoir in a natural cavity of the rock situated exactly beneath the N.E. corner of the original fortification (and at a depth of 18 m. below ground level).
     Clay pipes brought water from two springs to the East of the Acropolis into the reservoir.

Subterranean Fountain: Access to the reservoir begins from inside the city wall and leads down a covered staircase which traverses the full thickness of the wall and carries on, underground, outside the city wall, twisting and turning until it finds the rectangular reservoir which is 5 m. deep. The roof of the tank has a manhole filled with stones, loosely placed which acted as form of filter. It is at this point that the clay aqueduct ended filling the tank and part of the approach tunnel, according to the season of the year and the amount of water flowing from the springs. To prevent leakage from reservoir and lower end of tunnel, two layers of waterproof lime water coating had been given. This subterranean fountain which ensured water to the inhabitants of Mycenae who took refuge in the Acropolis, in time of war or siege, is one of the wonders of the mechanical achievements of the Mycenaean age.

Tunnels. In this latter section of the Mycenaean Acropolis are the two small auxiliary exits or tunnels. One served to permit sudden sallies by the garrison against a besieging force in front of the northern gate. The other led to a naturally fortified terrace which served as a look-out point. Below it stretches the impressive Havos gorge.

Houses A and B : On the N.E. extension the remains survive of two buildings which command the fountain and the exit tunnels. The foundations of the basement of House A together with fragments of some jars and other vases were found. Among the finds there was also part of one room and half a clay bath. House B is larger and rectangular. Its position suggests it could have been the habitation of the officer responsible for the safety of the underground reservoir and the water supply.

Northern Gate : In order to proceed from the N.E. extension to the northern gate, it is necessary to follow the path inside the Acropolis, which leads westward between the city wall and House C . At the N.W. corner of this house, the path forks one section leading to the entrance to House D and to the House of Columns, while the other leads west ending at the top of a stairway leading down into the inner court of the gate.

The northern gate has been built in a manner similar to that of the Lions Gate but is of different dimensions and, instead of a relieving triangle above the lintel, it carries two upright, rectangular slabs (one giving on to the outer façade and the other facing inwards). These slabs rest only upon the edges of the lintel at the point where the latter are supported by the pilasters. This is achieved by a slight hollowing out of the lower surface of the slabs so that they are slightly concave. In the case of this gate also, there is an inner court with a small shrine and an outer court with a tower on its western side.

Buildings of the N.W. Side : This side of the hill is covered in a motley of walls belonging to buildings of various periods, only partially excavated with results of such excavations as have been made not yet published. Building N , built above the Lion Gate belongs to Mycenaean days and so does a row of storerooms, built inside but along the city wall. Building M is also Mycenaean. This, according to one interpretation, housed the military commander of the Acropolis or fortress commander who was responsible for the northern wall. The storerooms were obviously an arsenal. This completes the tour of the interior of the Acropolis.

BUILDINGS OUTSIDE THE ACROPOLIS OF MYCENAE.

The Acropolis or citadel was inhabited by the King, the members of the Royal Family and the state officials. The remaining citizens dwelt in settlements outside the Acropolis, on the surrounding hills. These settlements consisted of separate groupings of houses inhabited by small groups of relatives. These houses, usually built close to one another, without partition walls, were separated by narrow, irregular passages.

Mycenaean Houses : One such group of four houses was excavated on the mound opposite the hill of Mycenae (known as the hill of «Panagitsa»). Another group of Mycenaean houses was excavated to the south of Grave Circle B . These are the West House , the House of the Sphinxes , the House of the Oil Merchant» and the House of Shields .

The «House of Shields» and the House of Sphinxes were thus named because, during their excavation, ivory tablets were found engraved with sphinxes and octagonal shields. In the cellars of the House of the Oil Merchant jars were found, set upon special hearths where fires could be lit to heat their contents. These installations and the aromatic plants mentioned in Linear B Script tablets found there strengthen the view that it was not the habitation of an oil merchant but rather a workshop for manufacturing perfumes and scented oils.

Mycenaean Tombs : Each settlement had its burial ground. Ordinary mortals were buried in rectangular holes hewn out of the live rock and covered with a stone slab. Earth was then cast upon this lid until flush with the ground. The dead were buried in a hunched position.

Towards the end of the 17th and during the 16th centuries B.C., members of the royal families were buried in tombs of the mid-Helladic cemetery which stretches across the western slope of the hill of Mycenae. The royal tombs become

The Treasury of Atreus
Le Trésor d'Atrée
Das Schatzhaus des Atreus

The Tomb of Agamemnon. (The Interior)
Tombeau d'Agamemnon. (L'Intérieur)
Grab des Agamemnon. (Das Innere)

Façade of the Treasury of Atreus
(reconstruction). ▶

enclosed in the two Graves Circles A and B . The latter is located outside the walls of the Acropolis and contains 25 tombs listed under the Greek alphabet from A to Omega . Of these, 15 are royal shaft graves while the remainder are simple, small, rectangular tombs hewn out of the live rock. As regards construction and dimensions, the tombs in Grave Circle A are similar to those in Grave Circle B . Burial rites were also the same. The precious ornaments and vases found in these tombs are exhibited in the National Archaeological Museum (objects made of gold, silver, copper, crystal and clay vases), as well as in the Museum at Nauplion (clay vases and tombstones or «stelai»).

From the end of the 16th century B.C., construction of the chamber and tholos type of tombs began. These chamber tombs are family tombs hewn into the sides of hills or mounds to a considerable depth. The section below ground is reached along a narrow, downhill, open-air cutting (dromos) which culminated at the entrance to the tomb or burial chamber. Access to the chamber was through a low entrance cut through the rock. Depending on the formation and hardness of the soil or rock, the chambers were of rectangular, elliptical, circular, etc. shape. The dead were either placed directly on the floor with the ornaments, vases etc. arranged around them or they were placed in pitçe dug into the floor of the chamber and covered with stone slabs. After burial, the door and outer access to the mouth of the chamber was closed with dry stone and the approach road was blocked. The hills of Mycenae are honeycombed with sets of chamber tombs. The Tholos tombs are royal tombs and form a more luxurious and stately version of the chamber tombs. They, also, have an approach road, a mouth to the opening and doorway with a chamber within. The difference is that the door, the mouth and the chamber are built with stone blocks, sometimes above ground level, in which case they were subsequently covered with earth to form an artificial mound, or they were set in a deep, circular excavation, cut into the side of a hill, in which case the approach path «Dromos» was almost level with vertical walls. Internally, tholos tombs were circular viewed from above and beehive shaped, built in the overlapping manner. This is to say that consecutive circular rows of stones were laid each circle extending inward slightly more than the row upon which it rested. This meant that, with each additional circle, the perimeter lessened until only a small aperture remained at the top which was closed with a single stone slab or lid. The door consisted of built up pilasters which rested upon a threshold, also of stone. These carried voluminous lintels, two or three times larger, depending on the depth of the mouth of the chamber or tholos . In the Mycenae area nine tombs have been excavated but they had been looted from ancient times. They date from 1500 to 1200 B.C. and can be distinguished into three groups which form the demarcation in the evolution of their architecture. (Ist Group, Tombs of Cyclopes, Epano Fournou, Aigisthus, 2nd Group, Tombs of Panaghia, Kato Fournou, Lions and 3rd Group, Tombs of the Daemons, Klytaimnystra, Atreus).

Treasure of Atreus or Tomb of Agamemnon : An impressive structure built around the year 1250 B.C. It was built into the side of a hill which was inhabited at the time (Panaghitsa hill), some 400 m. S.W. of the Acropolis. The approach path vertical with vertical sidewalls, is 36 m long by 6 m broad.

The sidewalls were built of stone blocks.

The surface of the approach road was overlaid with white clay and the eastern extremity was blocked by a low cross-wall of similar construction. At the western extremity of the approach path stands the monumental façade 10.5 m high. In the

Mycenaean Gold Mask   Masque en or Mycénien   Mykenische Gold-Maske

middle of this is an opening, tapering upwards. To left and right there used to stand a half-column of greenish marble set upon a low, square base and decorated with horizontal corrugated strips and a spiral. Above the aperture and the lintel there was a relieving triangle concealed behind a lining of multicoloured marble, decorated with horizontal strips, spirals and semi-rosettes (this lining has now been lost;nothing but a few fragments having been found). This lining or coating was flanked by two smaller and finer half-columns, similar to the ones below except for the fact that their fluting was slanting and spiral instead of horizontal and broken. The mouth is very deep (5.20 m). The threshold was half-way with the immense leaves of the doorway fitted to each side. The larger inner section of the chamber mouth was covered by a monoblock lintel weighing 120 tons. The «tholos» has been built of 33 concentric courses of stone blocks. At various points in the domed masonry, there are signs of copper nails which suggest that the interior had probably been decorated, maybe with copper rosettes. Into the northern side of the burial chamber, a rectangular sideroom has been hewn out of the live rock. This had originally been lined with thin stone slabs which were engraved. In the middle there had probably been a column or support for the roof lining. Long before Pausanias visited the site, the contents of the tomb had been looted. The treasure of Atreus forms a staging point in European architecture.

Gold cup. Tomb at Vophio
Coupe d'or. Tombe de Vaphio
Goldschale. Grab in Vaphio

Gold cup. Tomb at Vophio
Coupe d'or. Tombe de Vaphio
Goldschale. Grab in Vaphio

Daggers from the Royal tombs of Mycenae
Poignards provenant des tombes Royales de Mycènes
Dolche aus den Konigsgräbern in Mykene

Mycenaean Bull's Head
Tête de taureau de Mycènes
Stierkopf aus Mykene

NAUPLION

Nauplia, Nauplio, Anapli and Napoli di Romania were all names given at various times to present-day Nauplion in ancient times, in Byzantine days and in the post-Byzantine period. The legendary founder of Nauplion was Nauplios son of the god of the seas Poseidon and Amymone. He was considered to have been a great seafarer and an argonaut. One of his descendants and son of another Nauplios, king of Euboea, was the hero of the Trojan War Palamedes, executed by the Greeks themselves at Troy on a false charge of treason. Archaeological finds have proved that the area had been inhabited since pre-historic times. In historical times, Nauplia under the patronage of Poseidon with the city of Argos patronized by the goddess Hera as its rival, became party to the Kalavria alliance whose headquarters was the temple of Poseidon at Kalavria (island of Poros).

Argos gained supremacy after varying fortunes and Nauplia became deserted in the 2nd century B.C. only to be inhabited again, later. In Byzantine days, the monastery of Aghia Moni was built (12 century A.D.) close to the quarter of the town known today as Pronoia. Architectural members from some ancient temple were used in the building of this monastery. This was the site of the Kanathos spring where legend has it that the jealous goddess Hera used to bathe in order to regain her virginity. The modern city has been built at the foot of the rocky projections of great height, Palamidi and Akronauplia (also known at one time as Its Kalé) both of which are crowned by fortresses with walls stretching as far down as the shore. The Palamidi fortress was built, over the remains of the ancient Greek fortification, by the Byzantines, the Franks and the Turks. In older days, access was up 999 stone steps (or so it was said, though the actual number of steps is smaller). From the summit there is a unique view of the Argive Plain. A covered communication trench used to join Palamidi to Akronauplia which was, in fact, the ancient citadel of Nauplia. There is one more fortification in the area and this is a fort built on the tiny off-shore islet of Burdzi which lies a few hundred metres to the NW of the port of Nauplion. The Venetians fortified it. Nauplion today, with its picturesque lanes leading uphill from the sea, is strongly reminiscent of the Anafiotika quarter of Athens, at the foot of the Acropolis and, with some beautiful churches and stylish squares, retains much of the atmosphere of the first capital of the modern Greek state which came into being in 1827. (Nauplion served as the capital until the year 1834). Today, in Constitution Square, the old Turkish mosque brings back memories of the site where the first Greek Parliament sat («Vouleftikon») while in the barracks of the old Venetian garrison, with its arched doorways and windows, there is a small museum with interesting finds from the Argolis region.

Nauplia : The interior of the Palamedes fortress
Nauplie : L'intérieur de la forteresse Palamède
Nauplia : Das innere der Palamedes-Festung

The Bourzi fortress.   Sunset
La forteresse Bourzi.   Coucher du soleil
Die Festung Burdzi.   Sonnenuntergang

Nauplia : View from Palamidi
Nauplie : Vue générale
Nauplia : Blick von Palamidi

The Bourzi fortress.
La forteresse Bourzi.
Die Festung Burdzi.

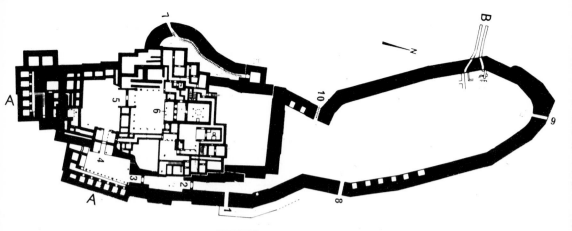

PLAN OF THE CITADEL OF TIRYNS
1. Main Entrance — 2. Outer Gate — 3. Inner Gate — 4. Great Propylaea — 5. Smaller Propylaea — 6. Royal Palace (Megaron) — 7. Western Entrance — 8, 9, 10. Tunnel Apertures — A. Syringes — B. Underground Springs.

TIRYNS

At a distance of 16 kms from Mycenae, on a small mound, are the remains of yet another Mycenaean citadel, that of Tiryns. Legend associates Tiryns closely with Argos and Mycenae. Proitos, King of Tiryns, who according to legend had the walls of Tiryns built with the help of the Cyclopes, was the uncle of Danaë, mother of Perseus (brother of her father Akrisios). Hercules, the greatest of heroes was a native of Tiryns and so was his cousin Eurystheus.

The fortified Acropolis of Tiryns (named the «walled one» by Homer) illustrates the zenith of Mycenaean art of fortification. As was the case with the Acropolis at Mycenae, it was built in three stages and received its final form in the 13th century B.C. It consists of the upper Acropolis (which is also the oldest) the Middle and the Lower Acropolis. Its walls enclose a total of 20,000 m². At certain points on the southern and eastern sides, the defensive wall attains a thickness of 17 m. At these points, a series of rooms have been built into the interior of the wall which give on to a corridor. The rooms are the famous «syringes» and probably served as storehouses.

Main access is from the eastern side. A narrow corridor begins from here through two limbs of the wall and is protected by two porches. The porches had doors which closed with solid wooden leaves. After the second porch, there is a large court with a small porch on one side which leads to the central courtyard of the palace. On the northern side of the central courtyard stood the palace proper which had a second storey and was richly decorated with murals. Around the central courtyard and the palace proper were various compartments of the palace. On the site of the palace proper, a Greek temple was built in the geometric era.

A second entrance exists in the western side. From this point begins an impressive stairway, protected by a semicircular projection of the citadel's walls crowned by a tower. Apart from these two entrances, there were three tunnel apertures in the lower Acropolis which were sealed in time of war. In the lower Acropolis two built-in water-collecting tunnels were found which led from inside the walled compound to underground springs and thus ensured the water supply of the Acropolis. Tiryns was destroyed by fire around the year 1200 B.C. There is much in common between the Acropolis at Tiryns and that at Mycenae. In contrast to Mycenae, however, no royal tombs were excavated here. It would seem, therefore, that there was a second seat of Government of the State of Mycenae, located at Tiryns and the latter must have been much closer to the sea than it now is (one and a half kms), after so many centuries of silting up of the bay.

The Gallery   Les Casemates   Südostgalerie

▲ Gold ring from Tiryns
Bague en or provenant de Tirynthe
Goldener Ring aus Tiryns

Fragment of wall-paintings from the Palace of Tiryns
Fragment de Fresques du nouveau palais de Tirynthe
Freskomalereie aus dem Palast von Tiryns   ▼

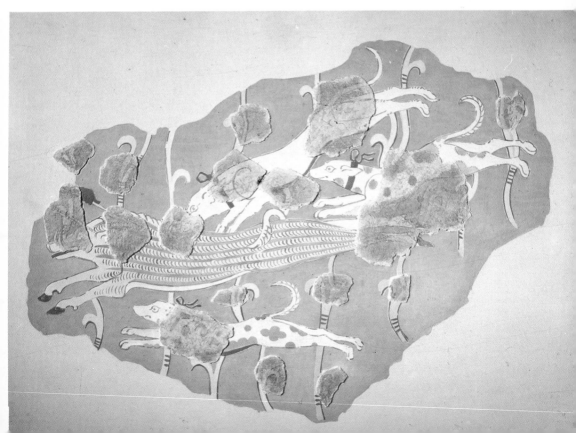

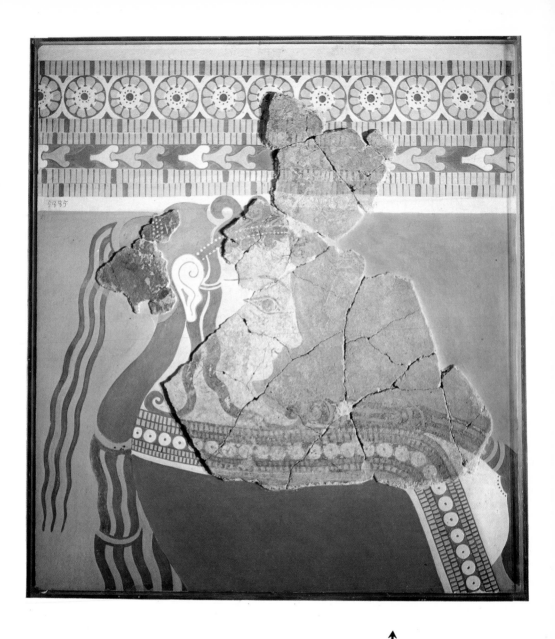

Fragments of wall-paintings from the Palace of Tiryns
Fragments de Fresques du nouveau palais de Tirynthe
Freskomalereien aus dem Palast von Tiryns

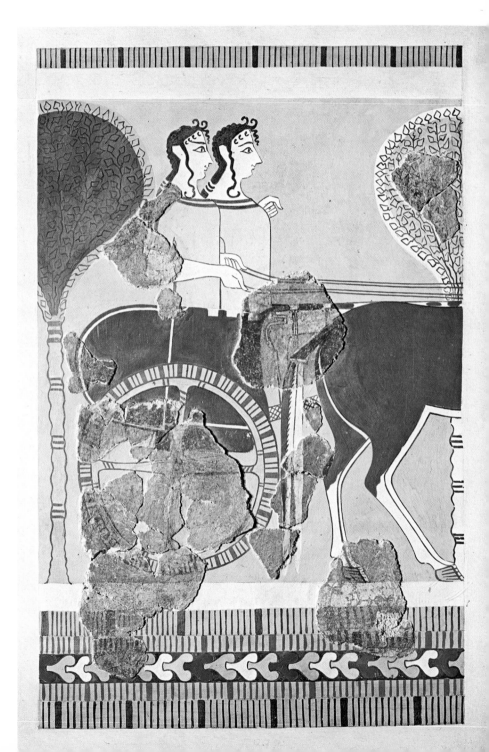

EPIDAURUS

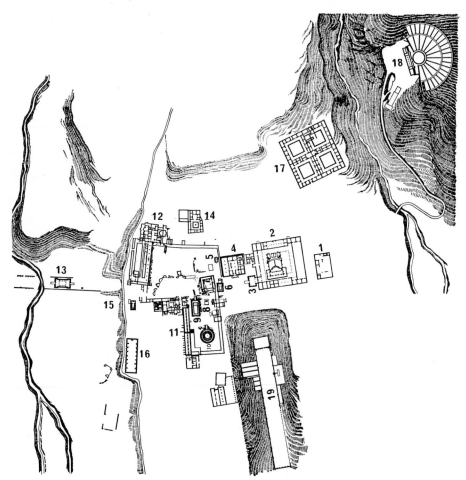

Epidaurus, Asclepios Sanctuary

1. Greek bath — 2. Gymnasium — 3. Doric Porch — 4. Arcade of Kotys (?) — 5. Temple of Themis — 6. Temple of Artemis — 7. Older Dormitory Arcade — 8. Altar of Asclepios — 9. Temple of Asclepios — 10. Tholos — 11. Abaton or Enkoimeterion — 12. Roman Baths — 13. Propylaea — 14. Sanctuary of Egyptians Deities — 15. Temple of Aphrodite — 16. Hellenistic Cistern — 17. Katagogeion — 18. Theatre — 19. Stadium.

Asklepios and the Worship of His Cult.

The Asklepios (also referred to as Aesculapius) Sanctuary, located in idyllic surroundings in the midst of a pine-clad valley between the mountains of Kynortio and Titthion, did not only attract the sick and deformed but also athletes, musicians and tragic poets who went there, every four years, to take part in the Asklepeia Contests which were held in honour of the deity.

The conduct of athletic contests on the site of the healer god is a relic of an older cult, associated with the hero Malos. As has been the case with several prehistoric heroes, athletic games were held around the grave of Malos in his honour. Later Malos was associated with the god Apollo who inherited the surname Maleatas. Thus it was that, in the area where the Maleates Apollon was worshipped, musicians appeared in due course of time, side by side with the athletes.

At about the same time when Malos was being worshipped at Epidauros, a local hero with healing capabilities, known as Asklepios, was being worshipped at Trikki, in Thessaly. From Homer, the most ancient literary source, all that is learnt is that Asklepios was a splendid physician, father of Machaon and of Podeleirios. In contrast, the more recent epic poet Hesiod gives information on the legendary status of the hero Asklepios.

According to this version, Asklepios was the son of Apollo and Koronis. During her pregnancy, Koronis was unfaithful to Apollo. The news was carried to Apollo by a crow and upon hearing of the behaviour of his beloved one, he was so upset that he cast a curse upon the crow, ever since when crows have been black. Koronis was killed by Apollo's sister Artemis but Apollo rescued from her burning body on the funeral pile, his little son Asklepios whom he carried to Mount Pelion and there entrusted his upbringing to the Centaur Chiron. It was from him that Asklepios was held to have learnt the use of herbs and prescriptions for various cures. When Asklepios began to practice his miraculous medical knowledge, especially his ability to revive the dead, he affronted Zeus who scorched him dead with a stroke of lightning. It would appear that it was upon the tomb of the dead Asklepios that the first form of his cult was born. It is likely that, in the early stages, Asklepios was worshipped in the form of the serpent since the serpent is not only the connecting link between the world of the quick and dead (through its ability to live both above and below ground) but is also capable, with its venom, of causing death or cure.

It is for this reason that, later, when Asklepios came to be worshipped as an anthropomorphic deity, the serpent remained as his permanent companion and symbol, even to this day when medicines carry the sign of the serpent of Asklepios. Therefore, the first Asklepeian sanctuary should have been located somewhere in the vicinity of the ancient city of Trikke in Thessaly.

Just when the cult of Asklepios succeeded that of his father Apollo at Epidauros is unknown. It is a fact that, early in the classical age (5th century B.C.) there is seen to have been a spread of the cult of Asklepios southward into Attica, the Peloponnese and the Dodecanese. Perhaps this was the result of certain epidemics which swept through Greek cities in the 5th century B.C. At any rate, Asklepios began to be formally worshipped at Piraeus, in Athens, at Sikyon, in Corinth, Epidauros, Cos, Rhodes, etc. In fact, in the 3rd century B.C., the fame of Asklepios had spread to such a degree that, when in 293 B.C. a terrible and fatal epidemic struck Rome, upon advice from the Sibyllists, a state delegation was sent to Epidauros which carried the god back to Rome in the shape of a serpent. Shortly after this, the first Asklepion was founded in Rome. Together with Asklepios himself, his daughter Hygeia was also worshipped. The worship of Hygeia began in the 4th century B.C. at Epidauros and thence was transplanted to other areas.

The sanctuary at Epidauros took shape mainly during the 4th and 3rd centuries B.C. A small temple was built in the centre to house the statue of the god being worshipped and around it were built various arcades and places of worship, a wrestling arena, baths, etc.

The Asklepion at Epidauros was not an organized hospital with medical staff such as existed at Cos. To the contrary, at Epidauros it was a sacred precinct were the priests and their assistants were no more than intermediaries between the patient and the god. The sick supplicants were first required to cleanse themselves in the waters of the sacred fountain after which they offered a sacrifice to the god on the altar outside the temple. They then resorted to the arcades round the temple in order to spend the night. At a given moment, after the priest had performed a kind of evening service, the «zakoros» used to tour the arcades and extinguish the oil lamps which had been burning since sunset. The sanctuary became plunged in darkness during the sacred night. The hoped-for cure would come with the miraculous aparition of the god during the sleep of the sick.

In some instances, Asklepios was supposed to have cured forthwith by the use of his supernatural powers while in other instances he indicated the cure to be applied. In the second case, it was the priests and their aides who determined the form which the cure should take. The god was held to be able to restore fertility to women who were sterile, cure ulcers, leprosy, dropsy, arthritis, constipation etc., and was even believed capable of restoring sight to the blind or one-eyed by rubbing ointment of his own preparation into the hollow socket of the eye. He was also believed to have caused hair to grow on the bare scalp of a bearded islander from Mytilene. The patient paid the fee after undergoing the cure. With the passage of time, when faith waned and patients began to doubt the miraculous qualities of the god, the priests began to apply more scientific medical methods, as witnessed in the text of an inscription found during excavations, which gave details of the cure for dyspepsia.

The cult of Asklepios lasted over a thousand years. Although, with time, the sanctuary degenerated into a den for impostors and charlatans and a nest of superstitions, it was nevertheless in the sanctuary of Asklepios that medicine found its cradle. It was for this reason that the doctors of the island of Cos, among whom the father of medical science Hippocrates, gave themselves the honorary title of Asklepiads.

ANCIENT SITE OF EPIDAUROS

Time has left very few relics of the most popular sanctuary of Asklepios. Following the small path to the left of the Museum, the visitor will come upon the first remains of the largest building in the sanctuary, a square structure 76.30 × 76.30 m. The «Katagogion» was a very luxurious, two-storey guesthouse with more than 160 rooms giving symmetrically on to four courts. West of the guesthouse lie the remains of a Greek bath and the vast Gymnasium with a porch in the Doric style

Reconstruction of the Asclepius sanctuary at Epidaurus.

at the NE corner. Inside was a court surrounded by a colonnade. In this cour_, in Roman times, an Odeon was built. Of this some of the tiers and the stage remain to be seen. The adjoining ruins are those of a later dormitory (the arcade of Kotyos).

From this point there is access to the sanctuary proper. At the SE corner, stands the minute temple of Themis and opposite this is the prostyle of the temple of Artemis (in the Doric style). On its northern side is the older dormitory arcade where the patients lay and awaited the visitation of the god in their sleep. This arcade was disused when in the 4th century the Abaton or Enkoimeterion (place of incubation) was built.

A path and inclined ramp, lead to the Temple of Asklepios. In the Doric style, it is one of the smallest of its kind in Greece. It was a peripteral temple (6×11) but, strangely enough, possessed neither rear vestibule («opisthodomos») nor an internal colonnade. It was built around 380 B.C. by the architect Theodotos. In the nave stood the ivory-gold statue of the god, the work of the Parian sculptor Thrasymedes. The floor was laid in alternate black and white marble paving. The door leading into the nave was adorned in wood, ivory and gold rivets, likewise the work of Thrasymedes. This most luxurious temple cost, according to an inscription, the exhorbitant sum of 100 talanta (equivalent to some $ 120.000). To the south of the temple stood the large altar of Asklepios.

Even more luxurious than the temple of Asklepios was the «Tholos», a fore-runner of which was the «Tholos» of Delphi. The «Tholos», also referred to in inscriptions as «Thymeli», was built some time between 360-320 B.C. by the architect Polykleitos Junior, who was doubtless the grandson or nephew of the famous sculptor by the same name who lived in the 5th century B.C. Together with the Theatre, it is one of the most noteworthy of the buildings. This «Tholos» or Rotundae stood on a stylobate of three steps. The circular wall of the cella was surrounded on the outside by 26 columns in the Doric style. The interior, to which access was from a doorway with two side-windows, had a colonnade of 14 columns with beautiful capitals in the Corinthian style. Both the carved and the painted decoration of the «Tholos» was exquisite. The floor was paved in black and white marble. Nothing remains today but the foundations consisting of three outer and three inner concentric walls. The three inner walls, which form a kind of small labyrinth, provided a secret crypt under the floor of the cella and probably housed the sacred serpents of the god which were bred there.

North of the «Tholos» stood two parallel arcades which mark the northern boundary of the entire sanctuary. By reason of the lay of the land, the more westerly arcade had two storeys. The upper storey came flush with the ground level of the eastern arcade. The two together formed the Abaton or Enkoimeterion, where the patients lay awaiting the nocturnal visitation of the deity. The arcade had two colonnades, an outer and an inner. The inner colonnade formed two passages along the arcade where there were benches for the patients to recline upon. At the SE corner of the Abaton, there is an ancient well where supplicants were required to cleanse themselves.

Continuing north, the visitor comes upon the remains of the Roman baths and still further north are the ruins of the magnificent main gateway or «Propylaea» which was the official entrance to the sanctuary. It was to this gateway that the «Sacred Way» from the port of Epidauros led. Close to this point, in early Chrisitan times, a Basilica with double aisles and a large atrium was built and its remains are to be seen today. East of the enclosure of the sanctuary, stand the remains of a temple dedicated to Egyptian deities but belonging to Roman times while to the west is a small temple of Aphrodite and a very large cistern of the Hellenistic era.

THE STADIUM :

SW of the sanctuary is the stadium, built in the 5th century B.C. This occupies a natural cavity in the landscape. It is 181 m long and the tiers of seats are either hewn out of the rock or built, according to the lay of the land. The subterranean passage connecting the stadium with the sanctuary and the absence of a sphendone to the track are reminiscent of the stadium at Olympia.

THE THEATRE :

The Theatre is located half a kilometre SE of the sanctuary, at the foot of the ancient Mt. Kynortion and is the best-preserved ancient Greek theatre. It was built by Polykleitos Junior who was also the architect of the «Tholos». Its cavea is separated by a girdle passage or «diazoma» which separates it into a lower and an upper cavea. The former was the first to be built and, later, the tiers of the upper cavea were built to enlarge the theatre. The lower block is divided into 13 wedges of staircases (tiers of seats) and the upper block has 23. The orchestra, approximately 10 m in diameter is circular with a floor of trodden earth. In the midst of this stood an altar to Dionysos, the «Thymeli». The chorus stood in the orchestra,

The Theatre
Le Théâtre
Das Theater

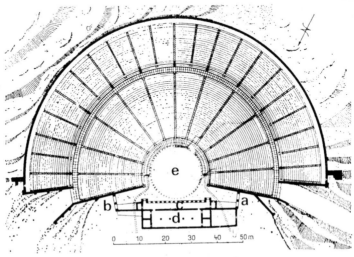

Epidaurus, Theatre
a, b. parodoi — c. forestage (proskenion) — d. stage (skene) — e. orchestra.

where the actors played their parts. Behind the orchestra was the long, narrow stage, on a raised level and directly in front of it the forestage which was, in fact, a decorative arcade formed with pilasters and half-columns in the Ionian style. The half-columns supported a cornice in the Ionian style and the intervening spaces were taken up with paintings. The forestage had a roof upon which actors very seldom played parts but it was the traditional place from which the «deus ex machina» invented by Euripides used to make his appearance. The forestage roof no doubt was connected to the second storey of the stage which rose a short distance behind it. The two ends of the stage include the pilasters from the Ionian style porticos which marked the beginning of the «parodoi». The Epidauros theatre is renowned for its acoustics, the slightest sound or even rustling of paper down in the orchestra being clearly audible from any one of the 14,000 seats. According to one version, the architect attained perfection in acoustics by placing hollow jars under the seats as they were being built, the mouths of the jars being turned towards the orchestra. In this manner it was said that he had achieved acoustic perfection by installing an infinite number of buffles. In the Theatre, now restored, the Epidauros Festival is held each year. Above the Theatre is the Temple of Apollo Maleatas.

The Stadium   Le Stade   Das Stadion

The Tholos of Polycleitus.
La Tholos de Polyclète.
Der Tholos von Polyklet.

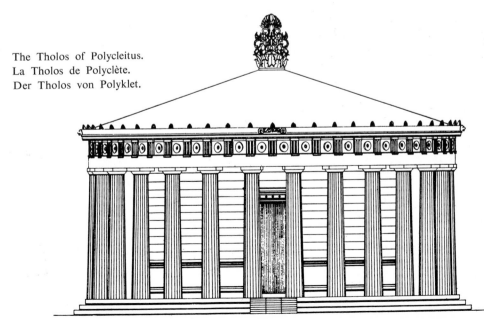

EXCAVATIONS AND THE MUSEUM EXHIBITS

The Asklepion sanctuary came to light in the 19th century when the Greek archaeologist Panayotis Kavvadias (1881-1887) carried out methodical excavations in the area.

Entrance to the museum is flanked by two columns in the Corinthian style taken from the remains of the inner colonnade of the «Tholos» and two in the Ionian style taken from the «Abaton». The first gallery of the museum displays medical and surgical instruments, numerous sacred oil-lamps, small clay offerings, Roman statuary and inscriptions with medical prescriptions and accounts of miraculous cures, texts which are of immense interest to the history of medicine and, at times, amusing. Other inscriptions refer to the cost of the temple of Asklepios and the «Tholos» as well as to details of their construction and decoration. The next gallery contains architectural members from several of the buildings in the sanctuary as well as votive and other sculptures. Most of these depict Asklepios while others depict deities in some way connected with Asklepios such as Hygeia, Aphrodite, Athena, etc. Of particular interest are the gypsum moulds taken from the statues decorating the ends of the gables of the roof. (The originals are in the National Archaeological Museum im Athens). They represent the goddesses Nike and Hygeia as well as two complexes of mounted Aurae or Nereides, these works being associated with one of the most famous 4th century B.C. sculptors, Timotheos, a pupil of Scopas. According to an inscirption, Timotheos undertook to supply the models for the statues of the gables of the temple and he personally worked on the end statues of the gable on one side of the temple. The Aurae have a completely ethereal appearance as their gowns stick fast to their bodies showing its outline clearly. A similar impression is created by the headless statue of Nike holding a partridge in her right hand (the symbol of health).

The piece closest to the style of Timotheos is the headless statue of Hygeia. The goddess is shown bending down in order to feed the sacred serpent which is uncoiling itself round her feet. Her spontaneous movement is shown to have caused her robe to slip off her left shoulder, thus uncovering her breast. All four end gables date back to 380 B.C., the gables themselves show on the eastern side a battle between Greeks and Trojans and on the western side a battle with Amazons. In the gallery at the far end of the museum there is a partial reconstruction of the entablature and certain architectural members of the temple of Asklepeios and other buildings. Some of the members of the Tholos are masterpieces, a partial reconstruction of this building being exhibited. The metopes of the outer circular supports (peristasis) are adorned with rosettes in relief while the marble cornice surface is decorated with lion's heads, blossoms with spirals of thorn in between. The decoration of the marble coffers of the roof exceeds the wildest fantasy, with hibiscus and rosebuds protruding in between in relief interspersed with thorn bush leaves. The interior of the Tholos had paintings by the Sikyonian painter Pafsias to complete the decoration. Among other pictures was that of Methe drinking from a transparent glass bowl in which her face was shown to be reflected. There is in the same gallery a capital from a column in the Corinthian style which was found close to the Tholos. The work performed on this piece was of such high artistic standard that it was believed by those who excavated it that it might well have been the model made by Polykleitos for the marble chisellers to copy when making the 14 Corinthian style capitals for the columns which formed the inner circle.

Ornaments of the
ceiling of the inner
colonnade (detail)

Ornements des caissons
du plafond de la colonnade
intérieure (détail)

Verzierungen der
Kassettendecke des inneren
Säulenganges (detail)

Sculpture from the temple of Asclepios at Epidauros
Sculpture qui ornait le temple d'Asclépios à Epidaure
Marmorskulptur aus dem Tempel des Asklepios in Epidauros

Corinthian capital.
Chapiteau Corinthien.
Korinthisches Kapitell.

Statue of Asklepios
Statue d'Asklepios
Statue des Asklepios

Making Friends on Beacon Street

Written by Dianne Bates
Illustrated by Margaret Power

Tilly and Tammy Hunter were sisters, and they had lived all their lives — more than seventy years — in the quiet old house where they'd both been born. They did everything together: the cooking, housekeeping, shopping, and gardening. They were as happy together as the very best of friends.

Then came the saddest time in Tilly's life — when her sister died suddenly in her sleep. All at once the old house seemed huge and empty.

Tilly did her best to go on doing the things that she and Tammy had done together, but sometimes she felt that she was just wandering from one lonely room to another.

Then one day, while Tilly was shopping, she found herself looking in a window at pictures of houses for sale. One of them showed a house that she recognized — a cozy-looking little house on Beacon Street. Tilly remembered how often she and Tammy had admired it during their walks together.

As Tilly walked home, she still had the picture of the house in her mind. "It would be just the right size for me," she thought. "And I *would* like to live where there were more neighbors."

Before long, Tilly made up her mind to move to the little house on Beacon Street — number 163.

It certainly was a busy street. People rushed by every morning on their way to work, and children laughed and chattered on their way to school.

Tilly stood at the front gate. "Good morning," she said to the hurrying faces.

"Good morning," the faces answered.

But everyone had somewhere to go; there was no time to stop for a chat. Soon the street was empty, and Tilly didn't see anyone else until the mailman came.

There were no letters for her, but there was a whole sackful of mail for the other houses. The mailman was in a hurry, and he couldn't stop to talk.

A woman came out of number 157, a few houses along, pushing a stroller. A little girl clutched her skirt and a small boy held her hand. Tilly hoped that she'd have a chance to say hello to the woman and her children, but they turned and walked in the opposite direction.

"Oh well," thought Tilly. "I suppose I could do some gardening. Somebody might come by." Tilly worked for a long time, but the street remained deserted. Then, as she stood up to go inside, PLOP, a rubber ball landed at her feet.

In front of her was a friendly-looking dog with short curly hair. He cocked his head from left to right, his stubby tail wagging crazily.

Tilly chuckled. "Where did you come from?" she asked. The dog ran to the ball and rolled it toward Tilly with his nose. Tilly picked up the ball. It had *Matthew* written on it.

"Who's Matthew?" she asked.

The dog's tail wagged even more crazily. He barked as if to say, "Stop talking and play with me."

Tilly threw the ball, and the dog ran to fetch it. He looked so pleased and happy with himself that Tilly laughed and threw the ball again . . . and again . . . and again. The dog looked as if he wanted to keep playing the game all day!

But Tilly was beginning to feel tired, so she decided to go inside for a nap. The dog followed her, and, after lapping up a bowl of milk, lay on the floor in Tilly's bedroom. Soon he was asleep, too.

That afternoon, Tilly stood at the front gate as children rushed past on their way home from school. "Excuse me," Tilly said, "are any of you named Matthew?"

"I'm Matthew," said a red-haired boy of about seven.

"I'm Miss Hunter, and I have your ball and your dog," Tilly said with a smile. "I took good care of them both." She handed the ball to Matthew.

"Thank you," he said. "The ball's mine, but I don't know who the dog belongs to."

"I think he's a stray," one of Matthew's friends said.

"It's nice of you to take care of him," said another.

Then off they all went. Tilly watched Matthew. He turned into the house at number 157.

It was getting chilly now, so Tilly went inside. The dog followed, his tail still wagging.

"You're such a friendly fellow," Tilly said. "I'd love to keep you, but I don't know if you really *are* a stray. Your owner might be missing you."

She led him outside to a sheltered corner of the verandah and gave him a pat. "You'd better sleep out here for the night, in case someone comes looking for you," she said.

For a while, the dog was quiet. Then he whimpered. Then he howled. And soon Tilly was patting him gently and leading him inside. "But you really will have to go home as soon as we find your owners," she said.

The next morning, Tilly stood at her front gate once again. "Good morning," she said to the people hurrying off to work.

"Good morning," they replied.

"Good morning," she repeated to Matthew and his friends.

"Hello, Miss Hunter," said a chorus of friendly voices.

After nine o'clock the street was deserted, and Tilly was alone. Even the dog had wandered off somewhere.

"I expect he's decided to go home to his family," Tilly said to herself, and she couldn't help feeling a little sad as she turned to go inside.

But what was this? The dog was running along the street. He'd come out of the yard at number 157 and was dragging something behind him.

A moment later the dog was dropping a red and white towel at Tilly's feet. He wagged his tail as if to say, "What a good fellow I am!"

"You little rascal!" Tilly exclaimed.

She picked up the towel. The dog snatched the other end. A new game — tug-of-war!

"No games with this," Tilly said. "It doesn't belong to you."

Tilly decided that she would wash and dry the towel before she returned it. At eleven o'clock, when it was clean and fluffy, Tilly put on her favorite dress and hat.

As she climbed the front steps of number 157, Tilly could hear the baby and the little girl crying. Tilly knocked timidly. Nobody came to the door. Tilly knocked more loudly. "Yoo hoo!" she called.

The young woman came to the door carrying the baby, its face pink and puckered with crying.

"Yes?" she asked, looking a little flustered. Then she smiled. "Oh hello, you've just moved in down the street, haven't you? I'm sorry that I haven't had a chance to come and say hello — but I've been very busy."

"So I see," smiled Tilly.

It was hard to be heard, with the baby and the little girl still making so much noise, so before Tilly explained about the dog and the towel she asked, "Shall I hold the baby for a moment while you look after your little girl?"

Smiling gratefully, the young lady gently put the baby into Tilly's arms. "Her name's Sarah," she said. Then she bent down to help the little girl, who was still crying.

The baby cried and wriggled for a while, but Tilly rocked it gently and hummed a tune that she and Tammy had always sung together.

Soon the baby lay quietly in her arms, blinking its tiny blue eyes at her. Then it blinked its eyes quickly — one, two, three — closed them, and was sound asleep.

The little girl, who was carrying a doll that had lost an arm, had almost stopped crying.

"My dolly broke," she told Tilly softly.

"I haven't introduced myself," the young woman said, looking much more relaxed now. "I'm Josephine. You've already met Sarah. This is Angela, and . . ." She looked around and then stepped into the next room. "And this is Karl," she said, returning with her little boy.

"You do have your hands full," Tilly said.

Josephine agreed. "There's Matthew as well," she said. "He's a great help, but he's at school now."

Tilly explained that she'd met Matthew.

"Matthew's been wonderful, especially since my husband has been in the hospital," Josephine said. "I was getting the little ones ready to go and visit their father when you arrived."

"I'd be very glad if there's any way that I can help you," Tilly said.

"Well," said Josephine gratefully, "I'm sure that Angela and Karl would love to hear a story while I feed the baby."

Tilly enjoyed the story almost as much as the children did — and she was glad to feel useful. Josephine couldn't thank her enough.

"I'm just pleased to help," Tilly said. "Anytime you need me, don't hesitate to ask. It's so nice to have new friends."

That afternoon, Matthew came to visit Tilly. He had some news for her. "I found out that nobody owns the dog," he said. "He used to belong to some people on the next street, but they moved and left him behind."

"Oh no, the poor thing!" Tilly said. "But he'll be all right now — I'll adopt him. And I'll call him Toby; that was my father's name."

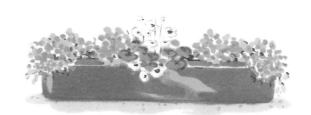

As Tilly was saying goodbye she added, "Would you please ask your mother if she'd like to bring all the family to visit tomorrow afternoon. I'll bake a lovely cherry cake, my sister's special recipe."

The next morning, Tilly found Toby in the garden when she went out to greet her neighbors on their way to work and school. He'd certainly had a busy night! By the front gate he'd left a pile of stolen goodies: a straw hat, a gardening glove, and a torn letter.

Toby looked up at his new owner, wagging his tail and looking very pleased with himself.

Tilly scolded him. Toby whimpered.
"Oh well, I suppose it's one way of
making new friends," Tilly said with a
smile. She picked up the goodies and
set off down Beacon Street to knock on
the doors of her other new neighbors.

"Do you think they'd all like to come
to our house tomorrow?" she asked
Toby.